WHERE WARRIORS MET
The Story of Lewa Downs, Kenya

EDWARD PAICE
illustrated by Sarah Elder

First published in 1995 by Tasker Publications
25 Burnthwaite Road
London SW6 5BQ

ISBN 0 9526113 09

TYPESET FROM THE AUTHOR'S DISC BY PTARMIGAN LTD
DESIGNED BY PTARMIGAN LTD
PHOTOGRAPHS BY EDWARD PAICE
ILLUSTRATIONS BY SARAH ELDER
PRINTED AND BOUND IN GREAT BRITAIN BY GRAPHIC IMPRESSIONS, LONDON EC1

To all those with Africa,

its people, and its wildlife in their hearts

And with my thanks to the Craig family, Anna Merz,

and Sarah Elder whose book this is

Table of Contents

Setting The Scene

"Oh for a lodge in some vast wilderness,
Some boundless contiguity of shade,
Where rumour of oppression and deceit,
Of unsuccessful or successful war,
Might never reach me more!"

William Cowper

LEWA DOWNS WAS, a century ago, a no man's land between the Meru people on one side and the Ndorobo on the other. The land was for the most part covered by dense bush, the domain of very large numbers of lion and rhino. But there was also some reasonable grazing, and natural salt deposits, and the more intrepid were not deterred from exploiting it, despite the dangers lurking unseen in the undergrowth. *"Lewa"*, meaning "men", commemorates them. It implies more than simply gender: it was only the bravest, the men amongst men, who would venture here. This was true in peace and war: the large number of traditional burial cairns on the land attests to the frequent encounters of rival groups of warriors in years gone by.

A bland description of Lewa Downs would label it a semi-arid cattle ranch. But this belies its fascinating prehistory and history, which are interwoven, part and parcel, with the history of Kenya itself. Today its activities are so much more varied than those of a pure cattle ranch. A dramatic shift of emphasis occurred as a result of the increasing importance of wildlife to the ranch and the drive to involve others, both near and far, in the attempt to conserve the natural habitat for a great variety of species. The aims of the Lewa Wildlife Conservancy grew directly from the experience gained during the first decade of the operation of the Ngare Sergoi Rhino Sanctuary, one of the first, and now one of the largest, conservation projects of its kind in the country.

Lewa Downs encompasses 40,000 acres and is situated 32kms north of Mount Kenya. This is real frontier territory. The bustling trading town of Isiolo is just to the northeast; beyond this the harsh territory of Northern Frontier District stretches as far as the Ethiopian border.

The landscape of the ranch is very varied, one of its great charms. In the south the altitude is 2000m, falling away to 1450m on the northern boundary. Now included within the Lewa Wildlife Conservancy the Ngare Ndare forest, in the south, is one of the most extensive dry cedar forests remaining in Kenya. Below it stretch the open and wooded grassy plains of the ranch itself, interspersed with steep river valleys and rocky outcrops and hillsides.

Each area has its own character and its own ecosystem. All depend, to a greater or lesser extent, on rainfall. The late rains in 1994 were long and plentiful, leaving the ranch green and lush, and with an abundance of food for all species. Other years are less clement. The potential hostility of the environment is just one of the challenges that have to be continually faced in trying to secure the success of every facet of the ranch's daily activities – from the survival of the cattle, to that of the rhinos, to the regeneration of the grasslands and forest.

This is the story of a very different African ranch in the shadow of Mount Kenya.

Prehistory

IN A WORLD where it is possible to communicate virtually simultaneously with some-one thousands of miles away, where you can fly from New York to London in three and a half hours, where horrific wars can be started and finished in less than the time that it took Mackinnon to make the first ascent of Mount Kenya, it is sometimes difficult to comprehend the vast timescale over which Earth has evolved. And how quick we, as human beings, are to destroy that heritage.

Sometimes it requires us to be in a particular, special, place to stop and think on such things, somewhere we can imagine our ancient forebears living, somewhere we are confronted by the vast changes that Time has wrought.

Most visitors to Lewa Downs are incorporating their stay within a concentrated tour of East Africa, not usually stopping for more than a few days. What many will not realise is just how long Man, and his ancestors, have been treading the same paths and sharing the same views. The straight answer to this is *half a million years*. To appreciate this can be rewarding in itself and can make you feel, perhaps for just one fleeting moment, that time is standing still.

There are no better places on the ranch for inducing this effect than those places which were clearly inhabited by our ancestors.

A LONG, LONG TIME AGO...

Although in many ways the last 25 million years are those of particular geological relevance to Lewa Downs, it all started long before that. Over six hundred million years ago Lewa Downs was part of a sea in which mud, sand and limestone were slowly forming sediments similar to those being deposited in the great oceans today. They were accumulating in what geologists call a "geosyncline", which is essentially an ocean trench, the one in Eastern Kenya being known as the Mozambique syncline.

Over a vast period of time the land masses on either side closed together as part of a process of continental drift, or "plate tectonics". The earth's crust is made up of plates which float on a hot, partially molten layer; the proximity of these plates determines what shape the surface takes; when they meet violently the effects can be spectacular. This movement causes both mountain ranges and, when the earth's surface is stretched, faults. The granite and gneisses (platy stones) that are so clearly visible around Lewa Downs today are the result of this sediment being slowly buried, over a period of millions of years, then heated to great temperatures and squeezed so that they eventually crystallised. Quartzite formed from sand, and constitutes the cliffs to the northwest of the Lewa swamp; marble evolved from limestone.

Such force was involved in this process that it forced up a vast range of mountains, with peaks of 7000m and more, stretching from the Horn of Africa to Mozambique. Today this range has obviously been worn away and what you see is the base of this once majestic chain.

THE RIFT VALLEY

The 6,000km Rift Valley itself, forging its way south just to the west of Lewa Downs, is the most pronounced and famous feature of Kenya's landscape. It was formed by the same process of plate tectonics, beginning about 25 million years ago. The rifting process, in case you should be under any illusion, continues today, and the landscape of Africa may be considerably different in another million years.

But two significant periods of geological upheaval occurred in more recent times to alter the landscape around Lewa Downs. Some 12 million years ago there were huge volcanic eruptions in the Rift Valley which spurted lava over the area around Rumuruti, about 80kms to the west of Lewa Downs. The vast plateau in the far distance to the northwest of the ranch, visible on a clear day, is the result of these eruptions.

Then, about 5 million years ago, and even closer to the ranch, the (then) 7000m volcano to the south erupted. With jagged peaks which even today reach a height of 5199m, that volcano dominates the view to the south – it is Mount Kenya, which gave its name to the country. The diameter at the base of the mountain is 120kms.

MOUNT KENYA

The Kikuyu believe that Mount Kenya, or Kirinayaga ("the place of brightness"), is the home, or at least a regular resting place, of Ngai (God). Ngai is all-powerful and influences all aspects of Nature: the sun, moon, stars, forests, rivers, rainbows, thunder and lightning. He determines the outcome of every stage of one's life. As confirmation of this belief many Kikuyu build their houses with the door facing Mount Kenya, hence the title of Mzee Jomo Kenyatta's book, "Facing Mount Kenya".

In 1849 Johann Krapf, a German missionary, was the first European to see the jagged peaks of Africa's second highest mountain. His stories of ice and snow on the Equator were largely greeted with disbelief at home. In 1883, however, the Scottish explorer Joseph Thomson, who gave his name to the famous waterfall at Kenya's highest town (Thomson Falls, 2360m), confirmed Krapf's sighting. But it is unlikely that any European had scaled the mountain before William Mackinnon's ascent of Batian, Mount Kenya's highest peak, in 1899.

THE VOLCANOES OF LEWA DOWNS

Although Mount Kenya is not far to the south, Lewa Downs' own volcanic activity is more recent, probably only a few hundred thousand years ago, and consistent with the time frame in which Man puts in his first appearance. The difficulties in dating precisely either the eruptions or Man's appearance mean that of course they may not have actually coincided, but it is a stirring thought that someone may have actually stood right on the spot where you stand now and watched these volcanoes erupt with majestic ferocity (and probably paid for the privilege of such a spectacle with his life). The remains of these volcanoes, with their black or reddish bubbly laval rock, can still be seen dotted around the ranch.

Nature hasn't only brought about enormous geological changes to the face of Africa but climatic ones as well. Indeed the two are often inextricably linked as part of the same phenomenon. As a more recent example of this linkage consider all the global climatic changes that were attributed by scientists to the eruption of Mount St. Helens in 1988.

PREHISTORIC WILDLIFE

Such were the conditions faced by the predecessors of the fauna that occur at Lewa Downs today. As far back as 20 to 25 million years ago there already existed a form of hyrax, an animal which looks like a large guinea-pig, one species of which was as big as an antelope. There were also the ancestors of the elephant, rhino, and a primitive form of giraffe. Predators were there too, species of cats and dogs, and in the forests bushbabies, apes and monkeys.

Prehistory

Between 10 and 20 million years ago the first bovids are thought to have developed, the antelopes, gazelles and buffalo. It is worth considering that it is the developments of this enormous, almost incomprehensible time frame that Man, in his wisdom, now so constantly threatens, partly as a result of the explosion of the world's population which has expanded from 1 billion to 4 billion people in less than 200 years, and partly as a result of the destructive weapons now at his disposal. But Man himself was of course a very late arrival on the scene.

THE HUMAN FACTOR:
EARLY MAN AND LEWA DOWNS

It was Charles Darwin who first expounded the idea of Africa as the Cradle of Mankind. He wrote in 1871 in "The Descent of Man" that it was "more probable that our early progenitors lived on the African continent than elsewhere". He has yet to be disproved in this respect. The three early, Stone Age, periods of Man's development in Africa are generally described as follows:

■ Early Stone Age, from 3 million to 100,000 years ago;

■ Middle Stone Age, from 100,000 to 15,000 years ago;

■ Late Stone Age, from 15,000 to 2,000 years ago, the beginning of the Iron Age.

CHRONOLOGICAL TABLE SHOWING STAGES OF HUMAN DEVELOPMENT

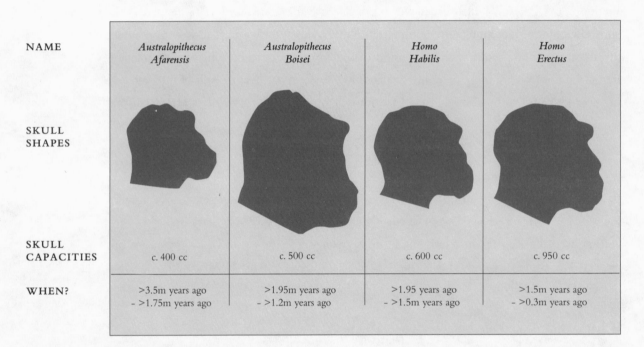

NAME	*Australopithecus Afarensis*	*Australopithecus Boisei*	*Homo Habilis*	*Homo Erectus*
SKULL SHAPES				
SKULL CAPACITIES	c. 400 cc	c. 500 cc	c. 600 cc	c. 950 cc
WHEN?	>3.5m years ago - >1.75m years ago	>1.95m years ago - >1.2m years ago	>1.95 years ago - >1.5m years ago	>1.5m years ago - >0.3m years ago

This century has seen many discoveries in Africa of hominid fossils which support Darwin's claim. Hominids are thought to have developed over the past 6 to 7 million years. But in seeking to identify separate phases of Man's emergence, there appears to be considerable overlapping and also many gaps in our knowledge. All research is dependent on not only finding relevant fossils, but also on there having been the correct chemical reaction at the time for fossilisation even to occur.

The term *Australopithecus* is derived from the Latin *australis* (southern) and the Greek *pithekos* (monkey). It is used to describe the oldest known hominids. Footprints of the oldest example yet unearthed, *Australopithecus afarensis*, were found in 1976 by Mary Leakey at Laetoli in Tanzania. They were dated at about 3.5 million years old. By 1.75 million years ago both *Australopithecus boisei*, or *robustus*, and *Homo habilis* were present at Olduvai, also in Tanzania.

It is not clear whether *Australopithecus* was the ancestor of *Homo* or whether both shared a common ancestor. *Homo* was bigger in stature, with a bigger brain, more upright stance and bipedal i.e. walking erect on two hind limbs.

By a million years ago *Australopithecus* had become extinct; *Homo habilis* had evolved into *Homo erectus*, with even more of the characteristics of *Homo sapiens*, and had probably pioneered the use of handaxes instead of pebble tools.

EARLY STONE AGE TECHNOLOGY:
PEBBLE TOOLS (PEBBLE TOOL OR OLDOWAN CULTURE)
HANDAXES (ACHEULIAN CULTURE)

Often the presence of our ancestors in particular places is attested to by discoveries of what was used in everyday life, as much as by fossil remains. Pebble tools were simple implements, small, and formed by striking one or two flakes from the core pebble to form a sharp edge. These, and the simpler flakes caused by striking one rock against another to produce a tool with no particular predetermined shape (such as those found at Omo in southern Ethiopia and at Lake Turkana in northwest Kenya) are the earliest known hominid-fashioned tools.

In view of the continuing debate about the age of both species the use of such tools is attributed either to australopithecines, or to their successor *Homo habilis*. What is certain is that the makers of such tools were hunter-gatherers, as is demonstrated by the contemporaneous finding of animal bones in the same locations as the tools.

Next, although overlapping for perhaps half a million years, came a more sophisticated means of fashioning tools, known as the 'handaxe' or 'Acheulian' culture. While the Pebble Tool Culture was unique to Africa, Acheulian handaxes and cleavers are also found in Asia and Europe. The name was coined after discoveries at Saint-Acheul in the Somme Valley, in France. Examples of Acheulian implements have been dated to as recently as 100,000 years ago, and as far back as more than 1 million years ago.

The tools were more precisely manufactured than had previously been the case, and were fashioned by *Homo erectus*, which existed between 0.3 million and 1.5 million years ago. Its brain, at 750-1000 cm^3 was larger than that of habilis; to give an idea of relative size, our own species, *Homo sapiens*', cranial capacity is 1400cm^3. It is still unclear whether *Homo erectus* was the immediate predecessor of *Homo sapiens* or whether there was a further clear stage of development in between.

LEWA DOWNS' ACHEULIAN SITE

"North of Mount Kenya, at a site called Lewa, Mr. S. Howard located another very rich site of Acheulian stage 4, and this site has yielded some of the finest examples of the long, asymmetrical type of handaxe that I have ever seen."
Louis Leakey
Munro Lecture, Edinburgh, February 1936.

With an uninterrupted view of Mount Kenya, and just to the west of one of Lewa Downs' streams, lies this 50 acre site which is strewn with evidence of a crucial phase in Man's development. It has been dated to about half a million years ago.

Acheulian handaxe technology moved through a number of stages, gradually becoming more advanced in the manufacture and application of the tools. One of the key indicators that a transition had actually been made from the Pebble Tool Culture to a new method of making tools was that an entirely new implement is found – the cleaver, which has a straight axe-edge rather than a rounded or pointed one. Many examples of these can be found at Lewa Downs, as the site is late Acheulian.

STAGES OF DEVELOPMENT OF HANDAXES

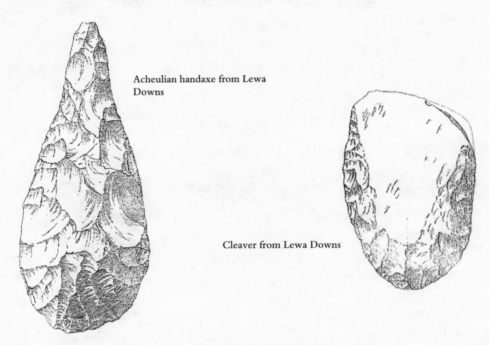

Acheulian handaxe from Lewa
Downs

Cleaver from Lewa Downs

Large pointed handaxes mark the earlier years and some small rather poorly constructed ovates. Gradually these ovates became more common and better made and cleavers developed an almost U-shape. Handaxes grew in size also to as much as 35cms. The tools, by the time they were being used at Lewa Downs are generally acknowledged as being very well made compared to the first ones to appear.

At Lewa Downs there are also a large number of "bolas" stones, spheroids, the use of which – as with all the tools – you are as free to imagine as the best qualified archaeologist, although we do know of their use as projectiles in more recent times.

One interesting feature of the Acheulian site is that, although bordered by water on one side, it cannot have afforded much protection. Were its inhabitants relatively safe from other hominids? If so, what about other mammalian predators? Did they have some means of stockading their campsite? What exactly did they use all these tools for – were some thrown as opposed to being hand-held? Why were they such specific shapes? And why was it that so many were left just lying around?

FIELD TRIALS

Although it will probably remain a mystery as to whether handaxes were thrown, you may – with such an implement in your hand – have some sympathy with a key argument used by proponents of this theory. Namely that if you struck something very hard with the tool you might well do your hand as much damage as the target.

Some interesting research has been carried out into the aerodynamic properties of the handaxe. Field trials have been carried out by, among others, Eileen O'Brien at the University of Massachusetts in the late 1970s. She found, with the help of two athletes, that if thrown like a discus the handaxe landed on its sharp edge in forty-two out of forty-five throws. The average distance of the throws was 31m. All landed within two metres right or left of the line of trajectory. This gives the tool a predictable record of an ability to inflict damage: if a number of hunters were all to throw into a closely packed herd of antelope the chances appear to be very high that a number of animals would at least be wounded and easily captured.

If handaxes were thrown it could also help explain why they are often found in great numbers, and near water, where wildlife would be more abundant. Such a method of killing would also have been startlingly similar to Man's preferred way of killing today – from a distance.

Prehistory

THE MIDDLE STONE AGE SITE

By 100,000 years ago Man had become altogether more sophisticated in his fashioning of tools. The rock shelter set into the hill about 1km to the east of the Acheulian handaxe site at Lewa Downs probably dates from this period. While the tools are similarly manufactured from lava, most of them are smaller blades, scrapers, chisels, flakes and cores. Small bones have also been found in the rock shelter which are likely to be the remains of meals, unless subsequently taken there by non-hominid predators.

The view of Mount Kenya is the outstanding feature of this protective nook. One thing is for certain: its inhabitants had already learnt to use places that afforded maximum protection – concealed from above and behind by the rock, they also had extensive views of the ground below and to either side. What did its inhabitants think of this great mountain to the south? What did they see on the plains below them? Did they venture to the fringes of the Ngare Ndare forest between them and the big mountain? And if so, how big was the forest, and how great the dangers that lurked therein?

There are other places of interest from a historical perspective at Lewa Downs, although none of them quite compare in significance to the two major sites described. While on a drive or a walk you may come across large mounds of stones. Many of these are burial cairns; although most belong to relatively modern times (the last few hundred years), it is still remarkable that so many have survived considering the continual needs for building materials and the inquisitiveness of much of the wildlife, such as elephant – who may may well consider that such things are a typically human ploy to protect a much-desired source of water. Mostly they are probably the final resting-places of Samburu warriors.

Others have actually chosen Lewa Downs as their final resting place. Among them are Tim Ward-Booth, a brilliant young helicopter pilot and veteran of the Falklands War, who assisted the Kenya Wildlife Service in the Mathews Range and was instrumental in training the security team at Lewa Downs. He was tragically killed in a car accident on the Nairobi-Mombasa road.

Newer than many of these cairns are the "bau" boards. Bau is a game with counters (pebbles) being moved around two parallel lines of beds, or holes. There are many variations on the basic concept which no doubt are caused by regional factors and the development of the game over time. The finest examples at Lewa Downs can be seen just off the track to the northwest of the swamp. The slabs of rock into which the boards are carved are surprisingly comfortable. Maybe the game was the best means of whiling away the hours while on the lookout for danger. Many of the slabs also have honing edges where a spear or knife was sharpened.

The Cast of Characters

ALEC DOUGLAS AND THE CRAIGS

IT IS AN INTERESTING thought that 1995 is the one hundredth anniversary of Kenya being declared a British Protectorate. Arriving on a holiday or for business today it is immediately apparent how much has changed in such a short time, and how many major events have taken place as Kenya moved, not always smoothly, from being an uncharted territory, to life as a British colony, to Independence, to a multi-party democracy. The history of Lewa Downs is intrinsically linked to these wider historical developments.

Until the 1880s Kenya, Uganda and a host of other African countries were virtually unknown to the European, except through the almost unbelievable tales of the first intrepid explorers. Indeed what is today's Kenya was certainly not a distinct geographical unit. Much of the coast was under the authority of the Sultan of Zanzibar; the interior was largely dominated by the proud and ferocious Maasai.

British interest in the area was first formalized in 1888, with the formation of the Imperial British East Africa Company by Sir William Mackinnon. Its aim was to exploit opportunities inland from a stretch of coast that he had rented from the Sultan of Zanzibar for the princely sum of £11,000 per annum. When Kenya was declared a British Protectorate, it followed a similar move in Uganda the preceding year and, without any consultation with the Maasai, the geographic boundaries of the future colony were drawn.

The Cast of Characters

The lure for the first settlers was the availability of land and the, at that stage highly theoretical, business opportunities presented by the start of the construction of the Uganda Railway in 1896. This was to run 582 miles from Mombasa to Uganda and was dubbed the Lunatic Line – there was no guarantee of any form of income whatsoever, devoid as the interior was of towns, plantations or industries. The capital cost of the railway, which was completed in December 1901, was a massive £5.5m. Although many did come to take advantage of the easy terms on land, it was not a deluge, and progress was brought to an abrupt halt with the outbreak of World War I.

After the Great War there was however a new wave of settlers and the Soldier Settlement Scheme was introduced whereby former combatants could enter a lottery for land in the colony. This scheme and the presence of a railhead at Thika were the key factors for many who settled in the vicinity of Lewa Downs in the 1920s. There was little evidence of human habitation at the time of their arrival, the Laikipiak Maasai having left the area in 1911.

The original ranch at Lewa Downs is still referred to as the "top farm", due to its higher elevation to the south of today's ranch. It was 2,500 acres of open grassland and was drawn in the Soldier Settlement Scheme by one Alec Douglas. He and his parents had arrived in Kenya from South Africa in 1912, and they originally farmed near Kitale in western Kenya. When World War I broke out he joined the King's African Rifles as a transport officer and was chiefly involved in the supply of oxwagons for the Tanganyika campaign, where Allied Forces confronted (or more often chased) their legendary German opponent, General von Lettow-Vorbeck.

The life of the early settlers was hard in the true pioneer tradition. Alec managed the farm singlehandedly while continuing to run a private supply business. Lewa Downs was bisected by the road north to Marsabit. As he left Thika with his wagons he would ride on ahead, allowing them to continue north while spending four or five days at a time at Lewa Downs and then galloping to catch them up before they reached their final destination.

On one such trip, he was camping at night on the Thika–Fort Hall (now Muranga) road. A young girl emerged from the bush with her dogs and carrying her rifle; she was clearly a bit shaken and explained that lions had killed her work oxen. She had managed to shoot two of them and wound another, but needed help to find the wounded one. Alec volunteered to pursue it and finish it off, and succeeded. The girl's name was Elizabeth Cross. She is reputed to have remarked to a friend: "what else could I do but marry the man?" This she duly did in 1922, in Marsabit.

Elizabeth Cross lacked none of her husband's fire and determination. The grand-daughter of a British Colonial Secretary, she had won the Military Medal as an ambulance driver in the V.A.D. (Voluntary Aid Detachment) in Flanders during the Great War. She too had subsequently drawn a farm in the Soldier Settlement Scheme. Unfortunately hers, at Makuyu, was not viable and went bankrupt, so she too had started her own transport business, carrying materials from Thika to Isiolo and the wilds of Northern Frontier District.

Their only child was a daughter, Delia, now Delia Craig. Soon after her birth the marriage foundered. After a spell managing the Llewelyn's farm, Ol Donyo, Elizabeth married Will Powys of Kisima, a neighbouring farm, in 1934. Will Powys had himself arrived in Kenya in the early 1900s and had moved to Kisima in 1925 from a farm in the Rift Valley.

Meanwhile, at Lewa Downs, Alec Douglas had few interests other than making his holding large enough for a viable living. He lived a very Spartan life in a thatched hut, wholly devoid of creature comforts. Every spare penny went into buying livestock or adjacent land as and when it became available. He just managed to survive the Depression, which ruined so many of his fellow farmers in the colony, partly because his frugal lifestyle ensured that he had virtually no overheads.

In 1945 he bought 18,000 acres just north of Eldoret in western Kenya, and moved there, taking with him 8,000 head of sheep for the new venture. He left Lewa Downs in the hands of his daughter Delia, who had spent World War II nursing in Nanyuki and Mombasa and then latterly as a wireless operator in Egypt. Her chance meeting with a young army officer, David Craig, from Devon, England on the hockey field in Nanyuki was no less unconventional than her parents' own first encounter, but perhaps the circumstances were marginally less dangerous. He still claims that it was his batman, Mzee Ben Ali, who first initiated the idea of courtship with the pragmatic observation that if he married the girl with the aeroplane "*we* could have a big farm." Following their marriage in 1949, they took over Lewa Downs full-time from Alec Douglas in February 1952.

Lewa Downs top farm was, by this stage, some 5,500 acres. There was also now a "bottom farm" of 13,500 acres, all slowly acquired over the years since Alec's arrival. Top farm supported 16,000 head of sheep, an enormous number considering the acreage, bottom farm just short of 1,000 head of cattle.

ONE LEOPARD CHANGES HIS SPOTS

Alec Douglas' success, as already mentioned, was largely founded on his frugality which saw him through the sort of disasters that make farming in Africa so precarious. He was also a forthright man who had strong views on many subjects – particularly lawyers and vets – whom he treated with a suspicion bordering on contempt. Even in his later years he was still to be seen dosing his sheep with a 10cc bottle, claiming that it worked better than the new-fangled syringe guns and wasted less. Seeing David Craig ministering to his 8,000 sheep with one of these, he told him he would murder the lot, as the medicine would go straight to their lungs. Concerned by the warning, the following morning David crept out of the house at dawn and satisfied himself that all the sheep were fine. But he was told that Alec had been to inspect even earlier and had set off post haste to Nanyuki to purchase one of these new-fangled devices for himself.

In the late 1960s he lived with a German companion who even succeeded in "getting him quite tidy": under her influence he once refused to go into the cattle boma *for fear of getting his shoes dirty. This was not natural behaviour for a man who had fought tooth and nail to make a success of life in his adopted country. Sadly, all the notes that he kept in the hope of writing his memoirs went up in flames in his hut at the farm near Eldoret. He died in 1972.*

The Mau Mau uprising, in the 1950s, was symptomatic of the changing tide in many parts of Africa where colonialism was waning, and nationalist sentiment grew stronger by the year. Although only 32 European settlers were killed in the uprising and some fifty troops, the toll on the Africans was heavy: over 13,000 men, women and children were killed. This was a harrying time, especially so at Lewa Downs in view of its isolation, and with small children and the safety of employees for the Craigs to worry about. Although trouble was limited there was one particular incident that many years later had a happy ending.

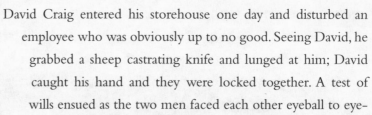

David Craig entered his storehouse one day and disturbed an employee who was obviously up to no good. Seeing David, he grabbed a sheep castrating knife and lunged at him; David caught his hand and they were locked together. A test of wills ensued as the two men faced each other eyeball to eyeball. The moment passed, a "discussion" began, and slowly both parties agreed that the best thing was for both to let go, and the incident would be forgotten. This it was, until twenty years later David went to a local *harambee* (fund-raising event) where this former opponent was treasurer. There was a question mark over a possible grant of funds to someone who was not trusted by many members of the committee. The treasurer, still unrecognised by David, refused the grant and turned to him, saying "after all, you and I *know* who we can trust". The penny dropped.

Throughout this period at Lewa Downs, as is still the case today, the Craigs farmed the land directly, dividing their time between top farm and attending to the cattle on bottom farm which was a four hour ride to the north. In 1971 top farm was bought by the Kenyan government as part of the response to population and political pressure on good agricultural land in the wake of Independence. The Craigs moved down the hill, built a house and set about the challenge of trying to do more with less. Some irrigation was introduced and they improved the cattle operations. The Craigs' daughter, Susan, established the ranch's Boran breeding strain and generally fine-tuned the herd, simultaneously linking it with a stud at the Eldoret farm. They also, as Alec Douglas had a generation before, took advantage of the

departure of various European neighbours to add parcels of adjacent land and, over time, to bring the ranch up to its current 40,000 acres.

Most of this additional land was considerably more marginal than the good grasslands of the top farm and therefore, from a resettlement point of view, the interest in its agricultural potential was less. All the purchases were sanctioned by the Meru Land Control Board. Soon afterwards the ranch near Eldoret which, like top farm, was prime agricultural land, was similarly bought by the government for settlement.

The vicissitudes of farming cattle at Lewa Downs in the late 1960s and 1970s were great, and making a go of it was a continual struggle. Sometimes trading, with up to 7,000 head of cattle, sometimes breeding from 3,000 head, sometimes with a dairy herd, there was always the need to be fleet of foot. Many new initiatives on such a ranch can be tragically undermined as the losses from foot and mouth disease and drought in the early 1980s attest to. The stock theft situation was also desperate at times, but this was brought under control over the course of two years due to an active campaign to put a stop to it, in which the Craigs' two sons, Ian and William, were instrumental. An extensive intelligence network was established, spreading far beyond the boundaries of the ranch. Cattle rustlers were routinely tracked north after each raid and then caught in a pincer movement at the places that acted as clearing grounds for stolen cattle. A reformed participant in these raids, now working at Samburu National Park, readily admits that the gangs largely gave up on Lewa Downs as a target, as they were caught so often! Other hazards included confrontations over large-scale illegal grazing and other matters, in which tempers on both sides often reached dangerous levels. Differences of opinion resolved, a number of former antagonists came in time to work for their former opponents at Lewa Downs. Sometimes the only salvation was that ultimately title of land is regarded as sacrosanct to both European and African Kenyans alike.

In terms of understanding how Lewa Downs evolved during this period into a ranch where wildlife and livestock are managed side by side, it is significant that Alec Douglas had always encouraged the presence of wildlife on the farm, and was imaginative in this respect. As just one manifestation of his interest, he bought 40 Rothschild's giraffes for his farm in Eldoret, at a price of 10 shillings each. These he built up to a herd of about 200 head, at the time the only viable population outside southern Sudan. After his death, the Kenya Wildlife Service took 22 head to Lake Nakuru National Park; now numbering some 60-70, this is the only such herd in Kenya.

The Cast of Characters

The welfare of wildlife then, as now, could often be at odds with the ranch operations. Even five decades after lions caused Alec and Elizabeth's first meeting, and four decades after the changing world of the 1930s described in Gerald Hanley's "Year of the Lion", this animal in particular was a threat. They were rampant and a persistent hazard to the cattle – much more so than the other large cats. Radical action often had to be taken in the days before all hunting was banned. Seven habitual cattle-eaters once had to be shot in a single night in the vicinity of the ranch. Lions, in a single night, could make the difference between a small profit or a thumping loss for the year. Accustomed to the easy pickings, they used to breed in profusion on the edge of the Isiolo Holding Centre, an area just to the north of Lewa Downs, where cattle were brought from far and wide to be quarantined before sale. For the lions it was tantamount to an all year round buffet of gargantuan proportions.

The balance over these three decades slowly shifted though, to the extent where wildlife as a land use, through deriving an income from tourism for example, is even more important than the remaining cattle herd. This has prompted a new management approach, undertaken by the Lewa Wildlife Conservancy.

Today David and Delia Craig are still fully involved in life at Lewa Downs, as are their sons Ian and William. Their daughter Susan and her husband have a highly successful dairy business in Nairobi. At the present count they have eight grandchildren.

THE NDOROBO

Many of the people living on and around Lewa Downs are collectively referred to as Ndorobo. They have a long association with the Maasai. Given that the Ndorobo are actually a large group of disparate peoples, with very different histories it is difficult to be specific about their origins. However, they do feature in the Maasai lore of the Creation, in which the Maasai are given all cattle, and the dispossessed Ndorobo are "sentenced" to a lifetime of hunting.

This paradox is a clue to the difficulty in defining the Ndorobo precisely: if cattle were taken from the Ndorobo and given to the Maasai, it does not seem tenable that the Ndorobo have never known how to look after cattle. The Ndorobo name derives from the Maasai term Il Torobo, meaning "the poor people", or some say "hunters": in Maasai terms the two would be synonymous. This can be taken by many Ndorobo to be derogatory and they will often prefer to be known by whatever sub-group they belong to. In theory it simply refers to the people as not being owners of cattle, the mainstay of Maasai society, without ownership of which it is impossible to command respect. Nowadays many Ndorobo are in fact cattle-owners, and it has been established that some Maasai will actually recategorise themselves as Ndorobo when something occurs to render unsustainable their normal cattle-centric lifestyle.

The origins of the term may well have been the result of at least three civil wars in the last century among groups of Maasai, in particular the Il Maasai and the Il Okiek, to which the Laikipiak Maasai belong (the Laikipia plateau stretches to the west from Lewa Downs). The split had its origins in the last quarter of the century when the *laibon* (spiritual leader), Mbatian, who gave his name to the heighest peak of Mount Kenya, died and left a disputed succession between his sons Lenana and Sindayo. The former remained with the northern Maasai, the latter had his powerbase closer to Tanzania.

Although this rift was healed in 1902, successive bouts of smallpox and rinderpest also took their toll on Maasai unity, as did the encroachment of European settlers. After most of their number moved, or were moved, further south in 1911–12, over time the remaining Laikipiak Maasai were eclipsed and dispersed among other groups across the plateau. Such dispossessed groups were among those who became known as Ndorobo as they often turned through necessity to an alternative, hunter-gatherer, lifestyle. Some also sought a lifestyle based on trade, such as ivory. Ndorobo can therefore be taken to be a term related more to the activities of groups that have been scattered by any number of afflictions, rather than a definition along strict tribal lines.

Both Swahili traders and European explorers encountered many such people in the highlands of Kenya, and the term Ndorobo came to be used to describe all of them regardless of their origins. Many of them still have a close relationship with either the Maasai or Samburu, perhaps a link that goes back to those origins. In many cases they moved to inhabit forests when defeated in battle, or in response to the effects of cattle-rustling or disease among their herds, hence the population in the Lewa Downs area, which is bordered by the Ngare Ndare forest to the south and the Mukogodo forest to the north. The people who live in and around the latter, whom many would refer to by the general term Ndorobo, call themselves Mukogodo Maasai. It may be that at some time all lost their cattle, but that is no longer the case. Today the Mukogodo Maasai have a varied lifestyle – rearing cattle, growing crops, and collecting honey (both for food and ritual). This is symptomatic of their adaptability over time, maybe originally in the face of defeat in battle, but also more recently by the banning of hunting.

THE MERU

To the south and mostly the east of Lewa Downs are the traditional lands of the Meru. Unlike the Ndorobo, which is more a collective term for many different groups of people, the Meru are quite a distinct tribe. One of the manifestations of this is their very detailed tradition of oral history, about which many studies have been made. It lives on today; even among sub-groups the same basic theme of their origins is evident.

Their ancestors came from a place called Mbwa, which some researchers have identified as Mbwara Matanga on the west of Manda Island, which lies off the north coast of Kenya. They were enslaved by a people known as Nguo Ntuni, the "red clothes", who may well have been Arab traders. Either as a precondition for granting them freedom or simply out of spite, their ruler set the Meru a number Herculean tasks. One such task was to make an ox (or elephant, according to another version of the story) defecate white, which they cleverly solved by making the poor beast eat vast quantities of white chalk. They resolved to escape and approached a prophet, known as Mugwe, to help them. He demanded the sacrifice of three young warriors which was duly done. The names of the three were Gaita, Kiuma and Mathetu, still the three main clans or *mwerega* amongst the Meru.

This done, Mugwe chose a leader, Koomerjoe, to lead them across the big sea. With the aid of a three foot magic stick, the *gitumo*, Koomerjoe parted the waters and the Meru crossed safely in three groups: the Njiru ("black", because they crossed at night), the Ntune ("pale", crossing at dawn) and Njaru ("white", crossing in daylight). They were pursued by the Nguo Ntuni but as the latter tried to cross the waters they closed again and all were killed.

The themes of this story show both Christian and Arabic influence. Progressively over the centuries those Meru who had escaped to the mainland pushed further and further into the interior eventually settling in the area to the east of Mount Kenya, known to them as Keremara "the mountain of splendour". Their own name, Meru, may well derive from some of the forested areas they settled in northeast of Mount Kenya, which were known to the Maasai as Mieru "the quiet and still place". There are many sub-groups of the Meru, including Imenti, Igembe, Muthambe, Egoji, Mwimbi, Chuka, Tharaka and Tigania. Their coastal origins are still reflected in the number of customs they have in common with, for example, the Pokomo on the Tana River (north of Malindi) and the Nyika on the south coast.

No account of who is on Lewa Downs at any one time is complete without mentioning the tourists, limited in number, who come to visit the ranch and support its activities in the field of conservation. Peter Hankin, an intrepid hunter-turned-guide, was the first to bring tourists to Lewa Downs. He had pioneered walking safaris in the Luangwa Valley, Zambia, in partnership with Norman Carr. At the time, in the 1970s, political interference in tourism in Zambia was so great that the business became virtually inoperable. Peter turned to Kenya. After a chance meeting with Susan Craig in a camp on the Tana River, he was persuaded to start Wilderness Trails, a safari company organising trips to Lewa Downs, where he was free to explore on foot. Peter was renowned for knowing every bird, tree and grass that one could hope to come across. In his late sixties he returned to Zambia on a short trip to supplement his income with a hunting trip. He was required to hand his guns in at the end, an order he complied with despite being concerned about a dangerous lioness that was known to be in the area. That same night the lioness came to the camp, raided the larder, and took Peter's mosquito net. The next night she took him. To die in this way was horrific, but even his son said that in a strange way it was a fitting end for a man devoted to Africa, and he died where he was known and loved. He was buried out in the bush. Locals turned up at the funeral from many miles around, and the drums beat for many days. The Wilderness Trails name has been kept in his memory at Lewa Downs by the Craigs, to whom he taught so much.

Another equally famous regular at Lewa Downs was the indomitable Digby Tatham-Warter, for whom Sue Craig also worked. He was a particularly keen naturalist and a pioneer of photographic safaris. Outside Kenya, where he settled in 1946, he was however best known for his conspicuous heroism in World War II, for which he earned the DSO. He was immortalised as the umbrella-brandishing company commander in Richard Attenborough's film about the Allied attack on Arnhem, "A Bridge Too Far".

The Rhinos of Lewa Downs

NOTICE

PRIVATE NO ENTRY WITHOUT PERMISSION

DO NOT LEAVE YOUR CAR

ALL RIGHTS RESERVED FOR RHINOS

L EWA DOWNS has always been a home for a great variety of mammals, large and small. The wildlife is part of the very fabric of this frontier ranch. They enjoy security, adequate fodder – provided that the rains fall – and in turn give enormous pleasure to the hundreds of visitors who venture up to the northern flanks of Mount Kenya to see them. Living amongst this complex web of animal species is however one that did not just arrive by accident. One which has been brought to the verge of extinction; one which without intervention would have been consigned only to zoos and museum cases. That species is the black rhinoceros – *diceros bicornis,* subspecies *michaeli.*

Lewa Downs is renowned for its conservation work with the black rhinoceros, aimed at stabilising the precipitous decline in numbers of this magnificent beast and, with luck and constant vigilance, its rehabilitation. Today the whole of the ranch and the Ngare Ndare forest on its southern border are gazzetted as a sanctuary to pursue this goal, alongside the management of all other wildlife and livestock. The area totals 61,000 acres. The battle to set up and enhance the sanctuary has been long and hard, and is a story of the determination of a number of individuals in the face of seemingly overwhelming odds.

THE PLIGHT OF THE RHINOCEROS IN KENYA

The black rhinoceros has been on this planet considerably longer than our own species, *Homo sapiens*, and until the past few decades they still occurred in reasonable numbers. Even as recently as 1970 some 20,000 or more roamed in Kenya, part of a population in Africa as much as three times this number. In the early 1970s many Kenyan National Parks were able to offer a virtual certainty of seeing them. Within a decade this had changed dramatically, and by 1990 Kenya's black rhino population numbered less than 400 and was apparently doomed. Tsavo National Park, which was once home to the largest population of black rhino on the African continent had two tiny pockets remaining with a total of 20 animals.

What brought about this decimation of one of the most remarkable mammal species was money and arms. Rhino horn has long been prized in the Far East for its supposed medicinal properties (not, as is often thought as an aphrodisiac, although it is used as such in parts of India). In North Yemen it was sought for the ornate handles of the *djambia* daggers, a much-vaunted status symbol. The new-found oil wealth in the Middle East in the 1970s combined with the ready availability of advanced automatic weaponry to provide both the money and the means for procuring large amounts of rhino horn for the financial gain of those involved. The price of rhino horn soared as demand continually outstripped the poachers' ability to supply. As the rewards escalated so the more unscrupulous in all ranks of society became involved. The network was extensive, ruthless and efficient.

The rhino's susceptibility to such an onslaught is self-evident: it is a large animal and, lacking many predators with the notable exception of *Homo sapiens*, it sleeps heavily. It is easily tracked, and not easy to conceal. As importantly, the horn is neither the size nor the weight of, for example, an elephant's tusk, making movement of the prize that much easier. Those trying to protect rhinos, when poaching started to escalate, found themselves too ill-equipped and too exposed to offer much opposition. This by no means deterred all from trying, but despite great determination and bravery their efforts were often undermined by colleagues and superiors. It was simply not feasible to fight an enemy within as well as without. The results were painfully obvious. Thousands of rhinos were being illegally shot and left in pools of blood, grotesquely scarred by the butchery which removed their horns.

Among those who did foresee the consequences of not responding immediately was Peter Jenkins, former Chief Warden of Meru National Park and subsequently with the Wildlife Department Headquarters in Nairobi. He was one of many who could see on the ground what was happening and repeatedly warned those responsible for Kenya's wildlife of the dangerous consequences of inactivity. Even in the late 1970s and early 1980s such warnings usually went unheeded. For the rhinos in his care in Meru it was soon to become too late: in 1977-78 the situation completely collapsed. From having a rhino population that was consistently estimated at over a hundred, none were sighted in 1979. This experience of the resources and insatiable demand of the poachers was one of the factors which led him, and others, to believe that sanctuaries were the only possible hope for saving the remnants of the rhino population. After retirement he played a crucial role in the creation of the Ngare Sergoi Rhino Sanctuary at Lewa Downs.

RHINO BEHAVIOUR

Black rhinos are often thought of as aggressive, irritable and stupid animals. How much of this reputation is based on their understandable terror of Man is open to conjecture. Their image undoubtedly suffers from the fact that they express themselves differently from many other endangered animals, with whom they compete for the interest and generosity of donors and the general public. They lack appealing eyes (only having sight of some 6-7 metres); they have neither the human characteristics of a gorilla or chimpanzee, nor the expressive trunk of an elephant. They are also hampered by lack of support in mythology: there is no rhino equivalent of Babar the Elephant, or Baloo in "The Jungle Book," to reach the hearts of millions of children. But this is largely because the rhino's means of expression are so little understood; and if we lack the ability to understand an animal then the tendency is to label it as stupid. Rhinos use their nostrils, ears, posture, and above all a complex system of exhalations for communication and expression. It is fascinating to have this explained by one of the team at Ngare Sergoi who have lived constantly with these magnificent creatures for over a decade. Young rhinos spend over four years with their mothers, and to watch mother and calf together, whether at rest or play, immediately dispels any thoughts that they have little social interaction. Anna Merz, the founder of the sanctuary, has also a multitude of examples of their intelligence from the use of their prehensile upper lip for opening gates, to their unusual ability not to panic in a crisis, for example when trapped. Our dismissal of their capabilities and fears is more likely a poorer reflection on our own species than on theirs.

The idea of using sanctuaries as a means of protecting the remaining rhino in Kenya was controversial. Many conservationists thought that they would be little more than zoos, with the animals losing their natural instincts and becoming the victims of static gene pools, with inherent dangers to the fitness and long-term viability of the species. Some also felt that enclosing them in areas, however large, would actually make them an easier target.

The point is there was no time for the luxury of such debate: it was quite clear to those who were familiar with what was happening in the field that without such radical action there would, quite simply, be no rhinos whose future to debate.

One of the factors that underpinned the arguments of those who were against sanctuaries was that WCMD (the Wildlife and Conservation Management Department, the predecessor of the Kenya Wildlife Service) still believed in the early 1980s that there were over 2,000 rhino in Kenya. Other authorities are on record as having believed at the time that the maximum number was 500. Even this turned out to be an overestimate: the WWF (World Wildlife Fund) census that subsequently took place counted just 350 in the entire country.

In the end those who were most concerned won the day. In 1983 a survey was carried out into the feasibility of establishing rhino sanctuaries, and a "Black Rhino Management Plan" was adopted by WCMD as policy. This led to vastly enhanced security arrangements being effected at Lake Nakuru, Nairobi, Meru, and Aberdares National Parks. The battle to save the rhino was on.

RHINOS COME TO LEWA DOWNS

A coincidence brought together Anna Merz and the Craigs at Lewa Downs. Anna Merz, a woman of great courage and determination, had spent most of her adult life in West Africa where, amongst many things, she was actively involved in a number of conservation issues, and became an honorary game warden (in Ghana). She and her husband came to Kenya to retire but she was keen to continue her work with animals. The story of the Craigs' offer of the use of land for a rhino sanctuary which she would fund, and the first decade of its operation is told in her book "Rhino At The Brink Of Extinction".

Working closely with the Craigs and WCMD staff, she had the courage to take an enormous gamble. Five thousand acres of Lewa Downs, called Ngare Sergoi, was ring-fenced with 20kms of the latest technology fencing. It stood 2.5m high. Security staff were employed, trained and housed; an aeroplane, vehicles, radios and other equipment were bought. But there was no guarantee from WCMD that they would be allowed to take in black rhino,  which are the property of the State (although the Director of WCMD, Daniel Sindayo, had given them encouragement). In other words they had to prove first that they could provide outstanding security, at a considerable financial outlay, before there was any chance that their project would be given official blessing.

With the infrastructure virtually complete, the test came when WCMD captured a male rhino in the Kitengela, adjacent to Nairobi National Park. They needed to find a home for him. The proof of the care with which Ngare Sergoi Rhino Sanctuary had been set up was there for all to see, and the area was no zoo: it was large, wild and completely uncontrived. At 9am on 11 March 1984 the sanctuary thus received its first rhino, Godot. This was the moment that all involved in the preparations had been waiting for (hence the rhino's name). The gamble had paid off. Godot subsequently fathered three female and one male calf before being translocated to Meru, where he tragically fell victim to the poachers.

SHABA'S CLASS

Anna and her team have never lacked in determination to try anything to promote the welfare of their rhinos. This begins with the care and doggedness with which information about outlying rhinos is followed up and they are tracked, captured and released in their new environment; it extends to the sometimes innovative methods that have to be employed either to save a rhino's life or assist in its acclimatisation. Thus Anna would take the baby Samia to bed with her, much to her husband's horror, to help the fledgling rhino to survive in the absence of its own ability to regulate body temperature. This was despite the problem that the little foster-rhino had with an explosive digestive system. One new arrival, Shaba, seemed not to respond to any attempts to calm her down when she arrived at Ngare Sergoi in March 1984. She was livid, and made every attempt to break out of the pen in which she was held pending release into the sanctuary. Her violence actually jeopardized her own well-being. That is until Anna hit upon the idea of reading to her. Every day for a week she sat above the pen and read aloud to the rhino below, often for several hours a day. Gradually, Shaba calmed down. Indeed this therapy had such an effect that, when the time came, there was actually some difficulty in getting her out of the pen. She had come to enjoy her daily stories. A more natural environment beckoned though and soon after she was coaxed away from the pen she was seen to mate with the bull, Morani. Her new life had begun in earnest.

Although National Parks had protected rhino areas, and although Solio ranch to the west of Lewa Downs had also taken in rhino, Ngare Sergoi was arguably the first rhino sanctuary of its kind in the world: privately funded and established with the specific purpose of protecting rhino and providing them with the conditions in which they could breed. There are now 39 rhino (22 black and 17 white) on Lewa Downs. The current inventory of the black rhinos is as follows:

Name	Sex	Arrived/born	From
■ SHABA	Female	25/3/84	Captured near Shaba
■ SHIMBA	Male	7/2/92	Calf of Shaba
■ JULIALI	Female	18/2/88	Calf of Rongai
■ KELELE	Male	7/5/84	Captured near Mweiga
■ JUNO	Female	9/9/84	Solio
■ JUNIPER	Female	28/6/88	Calf of Juno
■ STUMPY	Female	10/8/84	Solio
■ NYOTA	Female	1/12/91	Calf of Stumpy/Kelele
■ SOLIA	Female	1/10/84	Solio
■ SAMIA	Female	15/2/85	Calf of Solia
■ ZARIA	Female	9/3/88	Calf of Solia
■ SONIA	Female	23/8/91	Calf of Solia/Kelele
■ MWINGO	Female	16/2/89	Nakuru NP
■ KENU	Male	21/1/93	Captured between Laisamis and Marsabit
■ EKILI	Male	22/9/93	Ol Jogi
■ EPONG	Male	22/9/93	Ol Jogi
■ AMURI	Male	23/9/93	Ol Jogi
■ JAMES	Male	23/9/93	Ol Jogi
■ NDITO	Female	2/2/94	Solio
■ MELITA	Male	3/2/94	Solio
■ MTANE	Male	22/3/94	Solio
■ SAMUEL	Male	11/4/95	Calf of Samia

Note: Solio, Ol Jogi and Ol Pejeta are, like Lewa Downs, private ranches/sanctuaries. Another private ranch, Ol Ari Nyiro, has an indigenous black rhino population.

The Rhinos of Lewa Downs

The sanctuaries have given the rhino a chance. It is an important consideration when looking back over a decade of the day-to-day struggle to save them in various places in Kenya that it was not only their overall number but the distribution in former habitats which threatened their survival. The remaining outlying rhinos were so scattered that breeding at the rate now seen in the sanctuaries was simply inconceivable: some of the males that have lived at Ngare Sergoi during the last decade, such as Womba, Sabatchi, Kikwar and Kenu, and females such as Shaba were probably many tens of kilometres from the nearest other rhino, out of range even for an animal that can wander large distances.

But once brought to a haven, the natural problems that were common when rhinos roamed in greater concentrations do of course continue to manifest themselves. Although 20 calves have been born in the Ngare Sergoi Sanctuary, there are still the disappointments caused by fighting, the rejection of calves, and poor health. It is ironic that those who originally argued against sanctuaries on the basis of their being artificial have been proved so wrong. In seeking to provide a truly natural environment for these animals, the instincts and characteristics of the rhinos themselves sometimes work against their well-being, despite the efforts of well-wishers to save the species.

But the golden rule remains one of stewardship. In Anna Merz's own words: "The object of creating Ngare Sergoi Sanctuary was simply to try to keep some rhinos safe so that they could breed.. Although the rhinos are treated as wild animals and are generally not interfered with in any way, the poaching outside has been so appalling that each of our rhinos is very precious. If there is anything we can do to prevent it, we will not let them die.." At enormous expense security against poachers has been the key priority and one that, with minute-by-minute attention and dedication, the staff of the sanctuary have managed thus far to provide.

This is not an auspicious start to the morning. Pinned inside the car in view of Anna's house by a two ton rhino, who is pregnant and therefore inclined towards the temperamental. She gives a little nudge to the rear of the vehicle as if sizing up the opposition that may be offered by this funny tin animal, and the foul-smelling human contents within. As Samia has shown before, tipping over a car is rhino's play. She hates the smell of the city and makes her disgust plain to Anna when the latter returns from a trip to Nairobi. Anna arrives to rescue me, but as she opens the passenger door the end of a large horn pops in (and an even larger jaw) as curiosity gets the better of Samia. I froze. It is not the sort of encounter that one is used to dealing with every day. Some "constructive" chat from Anna, however, gets Samia into reverse gear and we are ready for the off. Anna raised this nine year old rhino from birth, as she was abandoned by her mother. She, and the big white rhino bull, Makora, have a particularly special relationship with their guardian. For Samia this means occasional supplemental feeds of her favourite lucerne. As we drive off towards her feeding spot at the bottom of the beautiful river valley that is Anna's home, my concern increases again at the sight, filling the rear-view mirror, of this enormous lady rhino following on behind with that rolling, bouncy gait that is almost comical in an animal of her size. Reaching the dry riverbed Anna walks towards her chatting all the way in soothing tones. Samia responds with little squeaks, snorts and rumbles. This is clearly one couple who don't mind conversation at the breakfast table. I watch in amazement as Anna treats ticks in the great folds of skins where the rhino's legs meet the torso; as she lifts her tail; as she bends down to meet her foster-child nose to nose for a little exchange of snuffles. It is all the more remarkable because Samia is totally wild, wild enough to be mated and to defend herself in the big wide world. Nobody else would be advised to go within many yards of her. As Anna turns away she simply says: "isn't she just beautiful? I adore her." It is hard not to agree....

LEWA DOWNS IN CONTEXT

But what of the success elsewhere? Lewa Downs provides one home for rhinos in Kenya, but the future of the species is being fought for on a broader front.

The official population figure is 430 black rhino in Kenya, an increase of 23% on the low point. This constitutes about 17% of the estimated worldwide population of 2550. The intensity of poaching in Zimbabwe in 1991/92, and again more recently, shows that there is hardly cause for complacency. Numbers there have dropped from about 2000 in 1987 to less than 300 now.

Of the 430 Kenyan black rhinos one third are on private land, although they remain the property of the State. In general, breeding rates are about 5% per annum, although in some cases this has been very much higher. About 110 rhinos are outside sanctuaries, 290 in ring-fenced or partially-fenced areas and there are reckoned to be 25-30 "outliers" (rhinos, mostly lone, that are neither in sanctuaries or national parks).

As detailed in the Conservation Strategy and Management Plan for the Black Rhino species in Kenya (KWS/Zoological Society of London, 1993) the immediate aim in the next decade is to enable the species to recover to number 2000, and an active programme of capture and translocation is designed to underpin this target. In addition to the case of Zimbabwe, Tanzania now has fewer than 150 black rhinos, and the species is extinct in Uganda and Somalia. A momentary lapse in vigilance would put Kenya's ambitions in jeopardy.

Ngare Sergoi Rhino Sanctuary, for its part in the strategy, has grown over the decade since its inception at considerable expense which has been privately funded. In 1987 a further 5,000 acres of Lewa Downs was made available to the sanctuary, and another 18.5kms of fence built. The extension opened in October 1988. Then, in 1991, a 52km fence was built to encompass the government-owned Ngare Ndare Forest Reserve to the south of Lewa Downs (which, as will be explained, had far greater implications than just making it safe for rhinos). Finally, a further 34kms of fence was erected in 1992 to give a total area (Lewa Downs plus Ngare Ndare) of 213 km^2. The completion of this expansion is estimated to provide enough land and food for 100 black rhinos. There is a 30m gap in the northeastern corner of the fence to facilitate the natural migration of elephants and other species.

THE BOYS IN THE FOREST

One of the immediate consequences of extending the fence to include the beautiful Ngare Ndare forest was that it opened up an ideal new habitat for the rhinos. Four males quickly took advantage of this and moved in. They all carry high-powered radio transmitters which are fitted quickly and with the minimum of discomfort. This is just one of the precautions taken to maintain their safety in an environment that is not conducive to round-the-clock visual contact. Tracking them here is an exhilarating experience, requiring total silence, a readiness to move through thick bush and forest stands — and a commensurate readiness to run extremely fast. For me, the exercise turned into one of tree-spotting as much as rhino spotting, constantly trying to keep within range of one that was easily scaled in a hurry, if James or one of his friends had their siesta rudely disturbed. The moments in scrub, where no trees presented themselves, made the heart beat noticeably faster and all the senses strained for the slightest crack of a twig; the scenery becomes an entirely secondary consideration.

THE WHITE RHINO

Lewa Downs is also playing a major part in the attempt to save one of the other four threatened species of rhinoceros, the white rhinoceros *(Ceratotherium simum)*. There are estimated to be as few as 6800 surviving worldwide, of which some 100 are in Kenya, all brought from South Africa which has in many areas become saturated.

Some contend that Kenya is not a natural choice for such a rehabilitation to take place, partly on the basis that the species was not thought to have ever been indigenous. But recent research seems to indicate that the white rhino did once occur in Kenya, and that the differences between the northern white (subspecies *cottoni*) and the southern white species are not as great as previously asserted. The argument seems slightly fatuous: if Kenyan parks and private ranches have the finance and the expertise there is little point in excluding them from trying to help this species as well. Solio Ranch has over 50 of these white rhinos, Masai Mara National Park some 20; Lewa Downs has the next largest population with 16 animals.

Apart from any other considerations the white rhino is a good "PR animal" for both species. They are also less accident-prone than the black rhino. If visitors and donors (understandably) wish to see the animals that they are either directly or indirectly helping to save, the white rhino is more likely to oblige. They tend to be less shy and to move in larger groups, and will often not be spooked even if you approach quite close (paradoxically it is also this that makes them more vulnerable to poaching). The white rhinos of Lewa Downs are:

The Rhinos of Lewa Downs

Name	Sex	Arrived/born	From
■ MAKORA	*Male*	1/5/84	Meru NP
■ GORORIKA	*Female*	7/12/88	Solio
■ RITA	*Female*	3/5/94	Calf of Gororika/Makora
■ MAREMBO	*Female*	8/12/88	Solio
■ N'JUKU	*Male*	14/10/92	Calf of Marembo
■ BARAZA	*Female*	12/5/92	Calf of Marembo/Makora
■ SUNGARI	*Female*	11/12/88	Solio
■ LARI	*Male*	19/3/90	Calf of Sungari/Makora
■ MARI	*Female*	6/6/94	Calf of Sungari/Makora
■ JAGWAI	*Male*	23/11/90	Solio
■ MILIONDA	*Male*	)	
■ UTHUMI	*Male*	)	
■ THALUME	*Male*	) All from Natal Parks, South Africa, 18/8/92	
■ UPONDO	*Female*	)	
■ NTOMBELE	*Female*	)	
■ Unnamed as yet	*Female*	22/9/94	National Parks of South Africa
■ Unnamed as yet	*Male*	9/4/95	Calf of Marembo

Although the creation of the Ngare Sergoi Rhino Sanctuary, which now encompasses all of Lewa Downs, was at its inception aimed at rhino protection it has had far wider consequences. The lessons learned about wildlife management and security have led directly to the creation of the Lewa Wildlife Conservancy ("LWC"), a new concept in ranch management in Kenya.

The Lewa Wildlife Conservancy ("LWC")

C AN PEOPLE and wildlife coexist? As the price for its protection can wildlife be made to pay? These were crucial questions facing Lewa Downs towards the end of the 1980s, and have determined the way it is now managed. This chapter describes how a proactive management policy was conceived and some of the initiatives being undertaken as a result. A number of them illustrate the extent of the involvement with related challenges beyond the ranch's own immediate boundaries.

Lewa Downs was, for over fifty years, principally a cattle ranch. But the relative importance of this activity has declined. The ravages of foot and mouth disease and drought in the early 1980s combined with the much greater capital requirements of the industry, mean that the herd size today has settled at about 1000 head. It is a registered stud for Boran cattle, a hardy breed that withstands the local conditions well, but whose numbers are on the decline. Today cattle are simply treated as just one of many assets to be managed and utilised, no more no less.

AN UNLIKELY COUPLE

I was astonished to see a graphic, and perhaps far from usual exposition, of the integration of ranching and wildlife at Lewa Downs. Driving past a Boran herd one day, it appeared to me that one of the steers just didn't look quite right. It was very large, even for a bull, and showed absolutely no inclination to move from the road. Eventually pulling alongside this beast, it showed itself to be....a buffalo! This versatile individual comes to join the herd, and one cow in particular, every now and then. Its docile companions have a remarkable effect on its temperament: one metre from a lone bull buffalo is not usually a place one would chose to be, renowned as they are for extreme aggression.

The Lewa Wildlife Conservancy ("LWC")

While the cattle herd has declined, the wildlife population has been growing dramatically as a result of pressure from poaching elsewhere and the increased encroachment, on natural habitats, of human habitation. This change of emphasis, and the experience gained in protecting the black rhino, called for the formalisation of new management techniques.

In April 1993 the Lewa Wildlife Conservancy was officially launched. The concept behind it is that of managing Lewa Downs as an integrated conservation unit, and providing advice and back-up for those neighbours wishing to pursue similar goals. This is not a new idea and is widely practised in southern Africa, perhaps most notably in the CAMPFIRE projects in Zimbabwe, but it is new for Kenya. The stated aims are:

- to promote conservation of the natural environment
- agricultural and pastoral development in harmony with wildlife conservation
- protection of water catchments
- conservation and expansion of natural forests
- to promote better co-ordination of land use and to minimise conflicts between wildlife conservation and management, and human settlement
- to provide for the protection and propagation of the black rhino both within Kenya and internationally
- to develop programmes for the purpose of protecting and nurturing other endangered wildlife and plant species
- to develop ecotourism as a means of supporting the above initiatives

Many projects have already been undertaken with such goals in mind, even before LWC was formally incorporated. Of these the setting up of the Ngare Sergoi Rhino Sanctuary was by far the largest undertaking, but others have been, in their own way, equally important.

Lewa Downs is at the eastern end of the Laikipia plateau which stretches as far as Lake Baringo. Until 1965 northern Laikipia had no elephant to speak of. Then one or two herds started to arrive, and numbers steadily increased as did the duration of their stay. A decade later there were over 2,000 on the plateau, largely driven there by the pressure from poaching (particularly to the north), and human settlement. Today Laikipia has the second largest elephant population in Kenya. The problem of dealing with these new arrivals, in an area which is itself largely given over to ranching and agriculture, has been substantial. Lewa Downs alone has over 200 of these elephant during and immediately after the rainy seasons, a population that is difficult to sustain. Elephant compete with other species, particularly the giraffe and black rhino for fodder, and are notoriously destructive; the long-term sustainable population at Lewa Downs is probably no more than 50-80. It was hoped that once poaching was brought under control and the CITES (Convention on International Trade in Endangered

Species) ban on ivory came into effect, they might return to their former feeding areas but so far this has not occurred. The elephant, in the meantime, have to be closely monitored. If nothing alters, the situation will have to be more actively managed, including the possibility of actually driving the elephant further north again. Many options are under investigation.

The Laikipia Elephant Project was set up, with initial funding from KWS, to oversee the surveillance and protection of the elephants; all ranches on the plateau work together to try to ensure the security of the elephants and minimise the damage that they do to small-scale arable farms on the plateau and its fringes. Some of the elephants are fitted with radio transmitters to help track their movements, assisting in protecting them and in understanding their current migratory patterns. No elephant has been poached in the area since November 1990, but if the ban on ivory was lifted or vigilance lapsed this situation could rapidly reverse.

ILNGWESI GROUP RANCH

The management of wildlife extends beyond simply dealing with the species in the immediate locality. For example, Lewa Downs' security staff take part in elephant surveillance in the Mathews Range twice yearly. All the team of the rhino sanctuary are on permanent standby to provide help and expertise wherever it is needed in the country. But there are many for whom the concept of wildlife management is a new one, and for whom the concept of wildlife as a potential source of income is equally new.

Ilngwesi Group Ranch to the northwest of Lewa Downs is one such place. Its owners are Mukogodo Maasai, and it has some 5850 inhabitants on 21,000 acres, mainly living off cattle ranching and subsistence crops. The land is extremely marginal, but there are good quantities of elephant, buffalo, zebra, giraffe, and some leopard and cheetah. For most people on the group ranch these animals were simply a menace: at best, they were potential disease carriers, at worst a threat to life.

With the assistance of LWC though an interesting and mutually beneficial project has grown up. As part of its inception Simon Kinyaga, the chief since 1978, went to the Mara district with Ian Craig to see just what was involved in making wildlife pay. He explains: "We are now incorporated, as of the end of 1993, and have a bank account. For us this was a very significant step. With the help of Ian Craig we are now able to make money from the wildlife on Ilngwesi and we can use that in a number of ways to help our people." As a direct result of granting a lease for camel safaris on Ilngwesi the residents had the income to dip their cattle against the ravages of East Coast fever for the first time. School facilities have also been upgraded, and investment proposals for boreholes and fencing for the protection of cattle are currently under consideration.

The co-operative is headed by a board but decisions as to how to spend their income are taken with all 448 family heads *in camera*; no proposal can be effected without 60% attendance, and the capital inflows and outflows are recorded for all to witness. Ilngwesi has thus added

another form of land use to the more traditional ones, and it is by no means inconceivable that black rhino will roam here too within the next decade. Such a move, as at Lewa Downs, would combine philanthropy with financial pragmatism: it would provide an additional habitat for rhinos, and also add to the portfolio of animals that Ilngwesi has to show tourists.

The Lewa Wildlife Conservancy ("LWC")

THE SITATUNGA PROJECT

It is true to say that both research and straight visual evidence show that Lewa Downs has more of some species of wildlife than it can cope with, principally those who collectively consume unsustainable quantities of grass and tree cover. But this does not mean that new residents whose habitats are equally under pressure elsewhere cannot be introduced.

One such species is the sitatunga *(tragelaphus spekei)*, a shy member of the antelope family, that lives in swamp areas. Their principal habitat in Kenya is at Saiwa Swamp National Park, off the Kitale-Lodwar road in the west of Kenya. They are difficult to see, partly because of the surrounding reeds of their natural habitats, but also because they live much of the time partially submerged. Their curious hooves are supposedly an assistance in stopping them from sinking when walking in the swamps, although not being webbed it can be difficult to understand this theory. In 1989, Lewa Downs was given permission, after study of their swamp by KWS, to take a breeding population from Winam Gulf on Lake Victoria. In 1990 and 1991 ten sitatungas were released in the swamp and have taken to their new home. Calves have been born and the current population is believed to number 14, although counting is notoriously difficult due to the secrecy of the species, and its habitat.

WAITING FOR SITATUNGA

An early morning spent silent on the observation platform beside the swamp, waiting for the faintest rustle that may indicate the approach of one of these wary creatures, is one of the great pleasures that Lewa Downs can offer the visitor. It is only partly due to the excitement of seeing a sitatunga, partly because of the very different scenery of the swamp and the backdrop of Mount Kenya. Before you, green reeds stretch away about a kilometre, surrounded on all sides by acacias; the colours all assume a much more vived hue in the clear morning light, the yellow acacias in particular contrasting with the clear blue sky above. Bees hum in the trees, the only sound to disturb the silence other than the quickfire tat-tat-tat-tat of a pair of Nubian woodpeckers drilling in a dead tree for grubs. Beyond the swamp the peaks of Mount Kenya rise in the distance, as yet unobscured by the cloud which will close around them as the temperature increases on the plains below. On the far side a family of warthogs, tails in the air, go about their business in their peculiarly assured fashion. Another family is on the move just below the platform, oblivious to the intruder above them. Occasionally a crash in the reeds raises expectations, but such obvious movement is either waterbuck or bushbuck. But turning once more to the little clearing below, there, right in the middle, having arrived without a sound, is a sitatunga fawn. Its mother appears to the left, also moving without the faintest hint of noise. Two crowned cranes fly overhead; a car can just be heard in the distance as work begins on the ranch. But nothing will disturb the excitement of this spying on nature.

A further study is currently underway to assess the viability of introducing the bongo *(tragelaphus eurycerus)* into the Ngare Ndare Forest Reserve.

GIRAFFE TRANSLOCATION

Overcrowding among the megaherbivores (elephant, reticulated giraffe and black rhino) has put a continual strain on Lewa Downs' ability to provide adequate fodder for all of them. Towards the end of the 1980s the problem with excessive numbers of giraffe reached a stage where it could no longer continue unaddressed. A variety of options were investigated, including driving a high proportion of the giraffe off the ranch and then fencing them out

(but this would have created an "island" environment), culling, and excluding the giraffe from certain habitats. By 1991 it was estimated that Lewa Downs had one of the highest concentrations of giraffe anywhere in Africa: 3 per km². The solution was a massive translocation exercise, the largest of its kind ever undertaken. Three hundred and fifty giraffe were rounded up with the help of a helicopter and vast holding pens, and moved to suitable areas in the Samburu and Womba areas to the north. This approximately halved the giraffe population and considerably eased the pressure on vegetation.

THE CONCEPT OF FENCING

Pressure on land in Kenya continues to increase markedly. This is a function of rapid population growth (circa 4.8% per annum) and the fact that 75% of the country, mainly in the north and east, is very dry and often affected by drought. In this matrix some 8% of the land surface, albiet largely land that would be difficult to cultivate, is protected land for wildlife. The *quid pro quo* is that this land provides tourist income, which is the country's second largest category of foreign currency earning. But many inhabitants never see any benefit from this revenue, and for those living on the boundaries of protected areas the wildlife is a constant threat to their everyday lives and ability to subsist.

Fencing at Lewa Downs began with the establishment of the Ngare Sergoi Rhino Sanctuary, but its purpose has now gone beyond the sole aim of protecting wildlife. The fencing of the Ngare Ndare Forest Reserve in 1992 is an example of how situations must be managed for the benefit of both man and beast. It protects the wildlife on the inside but also now protects the smallholders on its southern side. The impact of this was dramatic. One woman, not atypical, said it was the first time in 20 years that she had been able to feed her family from what they grew: it was the first season that their crops had not been raided by elephants.

While fencing may be controversial, the fact is that it is neccassary at Lewa Downs to protect the wildlife (particularly rhinos), and to protect the neighbouring residents from raids by megaherbivores. The 30m gap in its northern side allows migration, and this gap is much used, most notably by the elephant either side of the rainy seasons.

NGARE NDARE FOREST RESERVE

The forest is government land and as such is not *de iure* the responsibility of LWC. But LWC has helped in its protection and the protection of the people on its borders, partly because with so many calls on government funding this may otherwise have not been undertaken.

The Lewa Wildlife Conservancy ("LWC")

Lewa Downs itself is part of a much larger ecosystem that must be cared for. Ngare Ndare is 52km² of dry cedar forest, a remnant of forest that would once have covered much of the Kenya Highlands, and a beautiful area to walk in. Unless donors had been found to help preserve it, it was estimated that it would have been all but destroyed within the next decade. This destruction was being brought about by unsupervised timber and firewood collection. Under the initiative instituted by the Forestry Department and LWC to save it, local residents are given preferential employment, firewood collection is now kept within the bounds of the local requirement, and timber extraction and honey production likewise supervised by the Warden. The preservation of this ecosystem is important: it provides a home for hundreds of buffalo, up to 200 elephant, 200 eland, 300 waterbuck, mountain reedbuck, colobus monkey, leopard, warthog, bushpig, bushbuck – and of course rhino. This is in addition to a large variety of birds and vegetation. The immediate aim, as at Ilngwesi, is to enable the forest to generate tourist revenue to fund its conservation programme, to provide employment, and to protect the local people from wildlife.

LAND USE

Wonderful as it may be for visitors to Lewa Downs to see such great concentrations of wild animals, these do not live off nothing. Many species compete directly with cattle for food; others, such as the group of bull elephants that are present all year round are just plain destructive! The problem of ensuring that the land is able to support all resident wildlife is one that has increased steadily since Lewa Downs was able to offer relative security compared to territory to the north, where poaching was rife. In response to this a research joint venture has been established with the University of Pretoria to study carrying capacities at Lewa Downs; the results will be practically applied to ensuring that the ecosystem is sustained.

VEGETATION TYPES

The ecosystems of the ranch are many and varied. In a study made by Linsen and Giesen, in 1983, a total of 221 vegetation species were identified, belonging to 147 genera and 51 families. These included 32 species of tree, 37 shrubs, 39 grasses and 113 other herbs.

The open and wooded grasslands are mostly on black volcanic soil. The dominant grass species that this soil supports are bamboo grasses, pennisetum mezianum *and* pennisetum stramineum. *In the forest* themeda triandra *(red oat grass) and* panicum maximum *(buffalo grass) proliferate.*

With the exception of the dry cedars of Ngare Ndare forest, the main tree and bush species are acacias:

acacia abyssinica
acacia brevispica
acacia drepanolobium ("whistling thorn")
acacia lahai
acacia mellifera ("wait-a-bit thorn")
acacia nilotica
acacia senegalensis
acacia tortilis ("umbrella acacia")
acacia xanthophloea ("yellow fever tree")

The river valleys also support cyperaceae, *vines of* convolvulaceae *and* vitaceae, *aquatic* compositae, phoenix reclinata *(wild palm dates),* ficus *(fig) species and various types of* euphorbia, *most notably the distinctive candelabra tree.*

LWC, as opposed to Lewa Downs, now employs over 140 personnel of which 50 are highly-trained security staff. They are dedicated to ensuring that the ranch remains a safe home for wild animals and a constructive force within the local community.

The Animal Family of Lewa Downs

> "Here in our area there are many wild animals of different creations. Some of them are useful and important while others are destructive and very dangerous. All the wild animals have benefit to our nation. All the wild animals run away from their enemies. If you are a good one, you can avoid killing or hunting our wild animals so that our nation can have benefit and also us we can benefit from tourism. Please I want everyone to see that looking after our wildlife animals is work for everyone of us. When we save animals from their enemies, they thank us in our hearts."

Godfrey Muriuki Maingi
Mutunyi Primary School

Wildlife abounds at Lewa Downs so during the course of a two or three day stay you will be able to see a good cross-section of the larger African mammals. There is always the chance to see the **"Big Five"** (elephant, rhino, buffalo, lion and leopard), although lions are generally discouraged because of the cattle operations.

> "I was wondering about lion because when a lion catched a cow it can eat it all."

Faith Karimi
Mutunyi Primary School

A good field guide is a useful item to carry with you on your safari but if space is limited there are plenty available at Wilderness Trails or the LWC lodge. This chapter endeavours to put the great variety of wildlife in context.

Although the ranch is fenced, for the protection of the rhinos in particular, there is a gap in the north which is much used as a passageway to adjacent territory by other animals. Many prefer to stay for long periods at Lewa Downs; others come and go – most notably the elephant which tend to be more numerous when the rains come in April and November. The elephant herds, will spend much of the rest of the year to the north, in Samburu National Park, or elsewhere, such as on the Laikipia plateau.

Even when the larger herds of **elephant** (*Loxodonta africana;* Kiswahili: tembo) are wandering elsewhere, there is a core of bulls who remain at Lewa Downs throughout the year. Some of these are now stars of a recent BBC documentary in the "Natural Neighbours" series. Gilbert, the oldest bull, featured prominently, and treats his human visitors with the uninterested disdain befitting one of his seniority.

The elephant is one of the most impressive of the world's mammals, standing up to 3.5m at the shoulder. Their complex social life has been the subject of much study; if you are interested in learning more about their behaviour I would recommend Cynthia Moss's "Elephant Memories", one of the products of her many years spent studying them in Amboseli National Park. Understanding something of how an elephant is behaving, or expressing itself, at any given time adds considerably to the enjoyment of watching them.

The family groups that you will see at the time of the rains in April and November are predominantly female and led by a matriarch who will take charge of all matters from where the herd is to feed, to its defence. Males are generally expelled from the herd when they reach maturity between the ages of 12 and 15. Thereafter bulls will visit the females for breeding.

HURRICANE GILBERT

Gilbert is just one of the elephants who make Lewa Downs their home, but he is a most individual character. He first arrived during Hurricane Gilbert. Unfortunately his name is appropriate in more ways than one. In the almost daily routine of displaying his masculinity to anyone who will take notice he is extremely destructive. But what to do with one who is so much a part of the furniture? His curiosity extends to a fascination with all sorts of activities on the ranch, from watching the cattle being dipped to poking his trunk inside aeroplanes on the airstrip. His inge-nuity is also boundless: when he first arrived he wanted to follow cars off the property (a dangerous proposition at a time when poaching was at its peak). When he discovered his way barred by the electrified metal strands of the gates, he changed tack, believing that if he reversed through the gates he would not be pestered by the things. All to no avail, so he just took to uprooting the entire fence. Eventually, for his own protection and to curtail the worst excesses of his vandalistic nature, his tusks were removed (they are, of course, growing back). This led to yet more fame: in the famous burning of ivory stocks in 1989, carried out by President Moi in an effort to discourage poaching, there was one pair of tusks belonging to an elephant very much alive and not poached – **Gilbert.**

THE ELEPHANT PEOPLE

For many visitors to Lewa Downs, the experience is more than just a holiday. This was certainly the case for Jake and Suzanne Dutcher from San Diego. Their story is unique, but many who pass through have similar ones to tell.

The Dutcher's love affair with elephants began shortly after their marriage in the mid-1960s. They spotted a magnificent picture of a bull elephant in a shopping mall, but could not afford it. After two months of regularly returning to gaze at it, they decided they had to have it but, horror of horrors, it had been sold. They then decided never to suffer such disappointment again and to buy any elephant artefact that they could find. The collection grew and grew: statues, photos, paintings, wallpaper, carvings; their love of this mammal's form and behaviour turned into an obsession. They are now known among friends, and even people they have never met, simply as "the elephant people".

Jake always suspected that maybe there was an earlier explanation for his fascination than the incident with the picture. Sure enough, after ten years of collecting he was looking in an old trunk in his mother's attic and snuggled in the bottom was – a cuddly elephant! Although he had no recollection of it, his mother told him that he and the elephant had been inseparable during his third year.

In 1978 the Dutchers decided they simply had to visit Africa to see elephants in their natural surroundings. Through one thing and another this dream was not fulfilled until 1994; finally, after 30 years of marriage, they made it and were thrilled that one of their first encounters with the real thing was a meeting with Gilbert, who was predictably a "real hit". They took over 300 photos of the elephants during their stay, and their 1994 Christmas card aptly featured themselves alongside Gilbert.

"It was absolutely all that we had dreamt of, and then some.." was how they summed up the culmination of a thirty year dream. The next trip to Africa is already being planned…

The Animal Family of Lewa Downs

Other new stars of the screen are Roger and his friends, **reticulated giraffes** (*Giraffa camelopardalis* ss. *reticulata*; twiga). Giraffes use their very long necks to reach browse that is inaccessible to smaller mammals and mostly live off a diet of acacia. It never ceases to amaze onlookers how they can so readily and nonchalantly chew away at thorns. They can be seen all over the ranch (there are many hundreds), preferring the areas close to watercourses. They are also regular visitors to Wilderness Trails. At night, the loud thud of a heavy hoof and a crunching noise above the roof of your *banda* most likely means that Roger or his friends are having a night-time browse on the succulent trees of the garden. The reticulated giraffe differs from other giraffe races in being darker, and its coat pattern is of large squares and other geometric patterns separated by white lines.

The **black** (*Diceros bicornis*; faru) and **white rhinos** (*Ceratotherium simum*; kifaru ya majani) can be seen anywhere on Lewa Downs, although the blacks are usually particularly well hidden from the amateur eye. If rhino-watching is the main aim of your safari, game drives or walks can readily be organised with that goal in mind. The two species are heavily protected here and everywhere else that they still occur; their safety is the paramount concern of the ranch management. There are very, very few places left in Africa where it is possible to see both blacks and whites in the wild. At Lewa Downs you have a very good chance of doing just that.

The waterfall

Sitatunga

Gilbert and friend

Samia

Lewa Downs

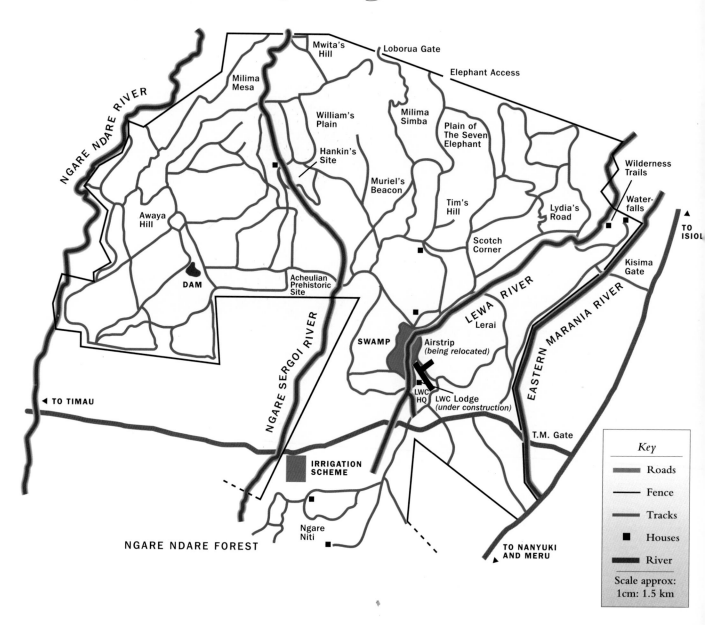

NGARE NDARE RIVER

Mwita's Hill

Loborua Gate

Elephant Access

Milima Mesa

William's Plain

Milima Simba

Plain of The Seven Elephant

Hankin's Site

Muriel's Beacon

Wilderness Trails

Water-falls

TO ISIOL

Awaya Hill

Tim's Hill

Lydia's Road

DAM

Scotch Corner

Kisima Gate

Acheulian Prehistoric Site

LEWA RIVER

NGARE SERGOI RIVER

SWAMP

Airstrip *(being relocated)*

Lerai

EASTERN MARANIA RIVER

◄ TO TIMAU

LWC HQ

LWC Lodge *(under construction)*

T.M. Gate

IRRIGATION SCHEME

NGARE NDARE FOREST

Ngare Niti

TO NANYUKI AND MERU

Key

	Roads
	Fence
	Tracks
■	Houses
	River

Scale approx: 1cm: 1.5 km

Roger

Baboon Rock

The Plains; Mount Kenya in the distance

Lewa River: dry season

The Animal Family of Lewa Downs

When you come across them it is easy to tell the difference between the two. The black rhino has a prehensile upper lip as opposed to the square muzzle of the white; the former is mainly a browser, the latter a grazer and the respective muzzle structures reflect this. Watch what they eat and how they eat it and this becomes clear. The "white" of the one species' name does not refer to its colour, although they tend to be lighter than the blacks, but to the Afrikaans word "weit" meaning "wide" and referring to that square muzzle. Whites are, as adults, considerably larger than blacks, have a distinct hump on their backs, and are much more likely to be seen in groups. The black rhino's ears, used by both species as one of their main vehicles for expression and therefore worth watching, are fringed. If you happen to startle a mother and her offspring, the white rhino mother tends to run with her child in front of her, the black rhino with it in the rear.

You may often see rhinos accompanied by oxpeckers, small birds which perch on the rhinos and help to rid them of parasites.

Of the big cats, sightings of **leopard** (*Panthera pardus*; chui) are a regular occurrence; the swamp, Ngare Ndare forest, and the cliffs between the swamp and Wilderness Trails are among their favourite spots. Anywhere you see yellow fever acacias is worth particular scrutiny. As with many of the cat family (*Felidae*), leopards are usually solitary, with the obvious exception of a female with her young. Nevertheless their ranges often display considerable overlap. This may be part of the explanation for the good fortune of one English family, who had never been to Africa before, and who on their maiden night-drive saw no less then six leopards together at Lewa Downs. Few who even live in Africa can claim similar good luck in their lifetimes.

Cheetah (*Acinonyx jubatus*; duma) also range the open grasslands. The cheetah is smaller than both the leopard and lion but much the fastest of the three. Capable of reaching speeds of up to 113kph in short bursts, it is a formidable predator. Obviously not as solidly built as the leopard, it has a smaller head, a more convex spine to assist with mobility and a shorter, rougher coat. This coat is covered in groups of spots; the pattern on the tail is one means of telling individuals. Females are usually solitary or accompanied by their young, but males often live in groups.

The plains and streams of Lewa Downs are the habitat for eighteen species of the bovid family which can be seen all year round, ranging from the very large buffalo and kudu to the very small dikdik and duiker. All except the species that are rare elsewhere as well, such as the sitatunga, are numerous. Antelopes belong to the bovid family (*Bovidae*), of which there are 75 species in Africa.

The largest of the *bovidae* is the **buffalo** (*Syncerus caffer*, nyali). Much of the terrain, with the exception of Ngare Ndare forest, is not as densely covered as one may normally associate with the habitat of the buffalo, but this does at least make walks through the bush rather safer than is sometimes the case: buffalos, especially lone males, are notoriously dangerous and unpredictable. With their magnificent horns and weighing up to 870kgs, these oxen-like mammals are usually seen in herds. Their sense of smell and hearing are very acute, but their eyesight is poor. The males take charge of the defence of the herd, forming a ring around the young facing outward, thus presenting a ring of sharp horns to any predator. The males are usually larger and blacker than the females, which also have more of a gap between the bosses of their horns. Surprisingly for such a stocky mammal buffalos are capable of speeds of up to 56kph, although their acceleration is poor.

The Animal Family of Lewa Downs

The *Tragelaphines*, the kudu and eland, are the next largest bovids, and the largest antelopes. The **greater kudu** (*Tragelaphus strepsiceros*; tandala kubwa) is a shy species, and therefore particularly rewarding to see. Usually seen in family groupings of 4-5 head one of the best places to look for them in the day is on hillsides, where they have adequate cover. Most of their feeding is done at night. Weighing up to 320kgs (in the case of the male) and standing some 1.5m high these are imposing and very graceful antelopes, distinguishable by the 6-10 vertical white stripes on the back. Only the male has horns which, when fully grown, will have two to three spirals. The record length for a pair of horns is 175cms.

The **eland** (*Taurotragus strepsiceros* ss. *pattersonianus*; pofu) seen at Lewa Downs are of the East African or Patterson's subspecies, and are slightly more rufous than their Cape cousins. They are considerably larger than a kudu, weighing up to 900kgs but share the feature of vertical stripes on the back, although these tend not to be prominent and are usually concentrated in the forward half of the animal. They have a large dewlap (fold of skin) under the throat; the male also has a tuft of hair on the forehead. Both males and females have horns, which are stockier than those of the kudu and have a much tighter spiral.

From the same family is the very shy **bushbuck** (*Tragelaphus scriptus*; mbawala or pongo); Ngare Ndare forest is a typical habitat for this species, which is almost never seen in open country. Colour varies with habitat, a natural response to the need for maximum camouflage; those seen in the forest are a darker brown than the more chestnut examples you may see elsewhere in less dense cover. Bushbucks stand a maximum of 90cms high and weigh up to 77kgs; they are usually seen alone. Both males and females have white patches spots and stripes on the body, but only the males have horns. Their tail is long and bushy with a black tip.

Very similar in shape to a topi, which does not occur at Lewa Downs is the **hartebeest** or **kongoni** (*Alcelaphus buselaphus jacksoni*; kongoni). The kongoni is a large antelope with a markedly sloping back, is light brown with a pale rump, and has a long thin head. It is a grazer of open country and grassland and usually seen in herds, varying in size from 4-15 head. Both males and females have horns, which grow outwards from the crown of the head and then backwards, forming the shape of a bracket standing on its tip.

Common waterbuck (*Kobus ellipsiprymnus*; kuru) and **Defassa waterbuck** (*Kobus defassa*) are numerous and, as their name suggests, usually seen close to sources of water. The area around the swamp is ideal for waterbuck which are easily seen there both by day and night. In the heat of the day these antelope look rather incongruous with their very shaggy dark brown coats, which are impregnated with an oily secretion. It is almost as if they would look more in harmony with the countryside of the Canadian Rockies. Measuring up to 1.25m at the shoulder and weighing as much as 200kgs, the only significant visual difference between the two species is white ring around the rump of the common; the Defassa has white patches. They are known to interbreed. Only the males have horns.

The **mountain reedbuck** (*Redunca fulvorufula*; tohe) is not often seen, as there are a limited number of suitable habitats at Lewa Downs. As its name suggests, the mountain reedbuck prefers mountainous countryside. Those that have been spotted at Lewa Downs have most likely strayed from Mount Kenya or the Aberdares. They are grey fawn, with a dark nose-stripe and mostly white underparts.

Oryx (*Oryx beisa;* choroa) are large antelopes of the *Hippotraginae* family. Their long, straight, backward-curving horns are a feature of both sexes. The open bushland areas of Lewa Downs are a good habitat for the oryx. They are often seen alongside zebra and Grant's gazelle, which are also numerous. Greyish in colour, they have a black stripe down the spine and flanks, distinctive black markings on the face and above the knees of the front legs, and a long predominantly black tail. The oryx is related to the gemsbok (*Oryx gazella*) of South Africa. Despite their sharp horns it is surprising that, when threatened by a predator, the normally pugnacious oryx will usually try and outrun it, rather than make a stand. Sue, David and Delia Craigs' daughter, discovered that this is not always the case. When her bull terrier gave chase to an oryx it turned and skewered the dog through its muzzle. Fortunately both dog and oryx survived the encounter.

The beautiful and graceful **impala** (*Aepyceros melampus*; swala pala) occur in very large numbers and are usually seen in breeding herds of females accompanied by a male, or in bachelor groups of males. The male is very territorial and can be watched chasing off would-be usurpers of his harem using loud snorts and raising his tail to show the white "flag" underneath. Competition amongst the males to breed is intense and herds of females will regularly find that their consort has changed. Both males and females have scent glands near their rear feet; the male also has them on the forehead and will use them to "mark" territory. Only the males have horns. Formidable jumpers, impala can cover 11m in a single bound.

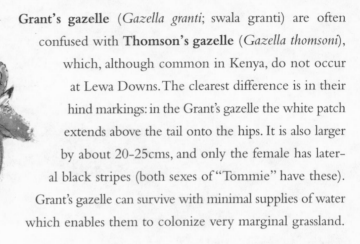

Grant's gazelle (*Gazella granti*; swala granti) are often confused with **Thomson's gazelle** (*Gazella thomsoni*), which, although common in Kenya, do not occur at Lewa Downs. The clearest difference is in their hind markings: in the Grant's gazelle the white patch extends above the tail onto the hips. It is also larger by about 20-25cms, and only the female has lateral black stripes (both sexes of "Tommie" have these). Grant's gazelle can survive with minimal supplies of water which enables them to colonize very marginal grassland.

One of the more curious-looking antelopes is the **gerenuk** (*Litocranius walleri*; swala twiga). Its Somali name – meaning "giraffe-necked" – is a pertinent description of its appearance and mode of eating. This feature, unique among the antelopes means there is no mistaking a gerenuk. When feeding it will stand on its hind legs and use the advantage of its neck to reach browse that is inaccessible to other large antelopes. They usually inhabit thorn-bush country and are even seen in deserts from Eritrea to Tanzania as they do not need water to survive.

In the swamp area it is possible to take advantage of the recently constructed hide when trying to observe the very shy **sitatunga** (*Tragelaphus spekei*; nzohe), which only occurs in a handful of habitats in Kenya. This breeding population, introduced from Winam Gulf, is now well-established.

Many of the smaller species of antelope are more easily spotted. One reason for their abundance is perhaps the relative absence of feline predators. The **steenbok** (*Raphicerus campestris*; dondoro) and **klipspringer** (*Oreotragus oreotragus*; mbusi mawe or ngurunguru) are members of the *Neotraginae* family of small antelopes, although there are considerable differences between the two species. Although both are between 50cms and 60cms tall at the shoulder when fully grown, the usually solitary steenbok is a reddish brown colour, with white under-parts, and has almost no tail. The klipspringer is much more compact and its greyer coat is rougher than that of a steenbok. It tends to be seen on or around rocky outcrops, and has a unique gait which gives it the appearance of bouncing on its blunt, almost cylindrical hooves. The ears are clearly bordered with black markings.

The **bush duiker** (*Sylvicapra grimmia*; nsya), also called Grimm's duiker or grey duiker is similar to the steenbuck but its neck is shorter, giving it an altogether more squat, low-slung appearance, and it is greyer in colour. It has a crest of dark hair. For many though, there is no more endear-ing small antelope than the tiny **dikdik** (*Rhynchotragus kirki*; dikidiki) with its big, dewy eyes. Standing no more than 40cms at the shoulder, dikdiks live in pairs and have a single mate for life. Often seen near roadways or peeping out from behind thickets they are usually grey to reddish brown with slightly lighter underparts.

One of the more exceptional features of Lewa Downs' wildlife is that the ranch is home to about 10% of the remaining population of **Grevy's zebras** (*Equus grevyi*; punda kanka). They are easily distinguished from the more numerous **Burchell's zebras** (*Equus burchelli*; punda milia) by a number of features. Their ears are very large and round, almost like radar dishes. Larger, and more mule-like in build, the Grevy's stripes are thinner and more numerous and the underbelly is white. In both species the stripe pattern of each zebra is different, enabling individual recognition. Zebras generally live in family groups with a single stallion, or bachelor groups. The teeth and hooves are used to try to fend off predators, the kick of a zebra being easily capable of killing a lion.

"WILDLIFE CALLED ZEBRA"

"This composition is about animal called zebra. It is a good animal and also neat. I love that animal because when I go to fetch some firewood with others in the forest, we see many zebras playing, jumping and going along the river banks while others are eating grass in the open field. Here in Mutunyi there are many wild animals like zebra, elephant and giraffe. Why I say zebra is good? Because zebra cannot go in the shamba *except when there is no grass in the forest. So it must go to find some food to eat, also to give her children. Some of them are male and others are female. Zebra eat grass and short trees. Its body is black and white stripes. It has four legs. Small ones are very neat and they like playing with their mothers."*

Purity Nkatha
Mutunyi Primary School

The Animal Family of Lewa Downs

There is a wide variety of primates including the fascinating lesser galago, or bushbaby, which is described in the section on nocturnal mammals. The most common are the **vervet monkeys** (*Cercopithecus aethiops*; tumbili), which are often a feature of meal-times at Wilderness Trails as one of their favourite spots is among the acacias on the steep slopes descending from the house to the stream. They are also numerous in the woodland around the swamp. Vervets are a grey or olive colour, with a white band on the forehead, black feet, and a black tip to the tail. The pale blue scrotum in adult males is prominent. More rare are the **patas monkeys** (*Erythrocebus patas*), large monkeys with a reddish, almost ginger, coat and white underbelly. The **Sykes monkey** (*Cercopithecus albogularis*; kima or nchima) is a regional subspecies of the blue monkey, although in its case "blue" is a misnoma as it tends to be greenish or reddish with black forelegs. Ngare Ndare forest is where you are most likely to see these monkeys, as well as the magnificent **colobus monkey** (*Colobus kikuyensis*; mbega) with its distinctive black and white markings, long coat and bushy tail. **Olive baboons** (*Papio anubis*; nyani) are easily seen, usually on the ground and in, or close to, some good cover. One spot where they are frequently seen is the springs, where they may well be scattered across the road, casually retreating into the woods if disturbed, and becoming quite invisible. They are very intelligent, but also very dangerous if agitated. As with monkeys, to feed them is to invite trouble. Many baboon species have "broken" tails i.e. they curve upwards before downwards. Males are considerably larger than females; if in oestrus the latter have large pink swellings on their rear quarters. Baboons' social behaviour is complex and interesting to watch, whether it be the ritualistic grooming, or a young one riding on its mother's back like a jockey.

Two species of **jackal** can be seen, the **black-backed** (*Canis mesomelas*; bweha) and the **side-striped** (*Canis adustus*; bweha). Resembling a cross between a fox and a wild dog, they favour open savanna and woodland. Both species are a similar size (about 40cms high). The side-striped is greyer and has a pale stripe along its flank and across the back; the black-backed is more reddish but with a black back that can look almost flecked with silver hair. These are very cunning creatures and a persistent menace to farmers.

Spotted (*Crocuta crocuta*; fisi) and **striped** (*Hyaena hyaena*; fisi) **hyaenas** are also occasionally seen, although like the jackals they are not easily compatible with ranching. Both are powerful scavengers, although quite capable of bringing down large prey such as zebras if working as a pack. Seemingly fearless when in such a group, they have even been known to attack humans. The mocking hyaena laugh is a common sound at nightfall in Africa. Hyaenas often rest or hide young in dens or old aardvark burrows.

Amongst the many rocky outcrops one may see the curious hyraxes at work or play. The hyrax is the closest relative of the elephant, a fact which can be difficult to credit. The **rock hyrax** (*Procavia capensis*; pimbe) is like a large brown rat or guinea-pig; the **bush hyrax** (*Heterohyrax brusei*; perere) is smaller and greyer. The two species will often live side by side. When accustomed to humans they become quite tame and are kept as pets in some parts of Africa.

Other familiar sights of the African bush that always fascinate are the **Somali** and **Maasai ostriches** (*Struthio camelus;* mbuni), the **African** or **Crawshay's hare** (*Lepus crawshayi*; sungura) and the **warthog** (*Phacochoerus aethiopicus*; ngiri). The ostrich is a bird, not a mammal, but as the world's largest bird – and one that doesn't fly – it falls more into the popular imagination with the larger mammals than with birds. The males are black, the females browner in colour. During the breeding season the necks and thighs of the former turn a striking pink. Their courtship displays are not to be missed. The warthog is a favourite with animal spotters too, busying hither and thither with its tail in the air, kneeling to drink, snuffling out food or grooming itself.

The Animal Family of Lewa Downs

.....AND BY NIGHT

IN MANY NATIONAL PARKS and Reserves in Africa driving at night is not allowed. Such a restriction is an absolute necessity when tourists are numerous in order to protect the animals' way of life and the environment. At Lewa Downs, however, night drives are possible as visitors are less numerous. This affords the magical opportunity to experience at close quarters a different world, that of African wildlife by night. The sounds, sights and smells of the African night are like nowhere else. With luck and sharp eyesight there is an opportunity to see some of the mammals whose activity is primarily confined to the hours of darkness.

Often the first "sight" of an animal will be nothing more definitive than the reflection of its eyes in the beam of the headlamps or spotlight; learning who's who from their eyes alone is part of the fun. Most species show no fear of the light so it is usually possible to approach close enough to see what is behind the glint of the eyes. But some of the nocturnal mammals are extremely shy; all the greater the satisfaction of meeting them too.

The **aardwolf** (*Proteles cristatus*; fisi ndogo) is a very elusive animal that bears many similarities to a striped hyaena – it is a member of the hyaena family (*Hyaenidae*). It is however altogether smaller, particularly in the head. Its Afrikaans name "maanhaarjakkals" gives a more accurate indication of one of its most prominent features than its common name: it has a mane that runs along the spine from neck to tail. This is erected when the aardwolf is alarmed or threatened to make it appear more foreboding. It is buff to reddish-brown in colour, with lighter underparts; there are vertical brown stripes on the torso. The feet, muzzle, backs of the ears, spinal stripe and outer tail are all black. Feeding mainly on insects, the aardwolf can consume up to a quarter of a million in a single night.

Equally elusive is the prehistoric-looking **aardvark** or antbear (*Orycteropus afer*, muhanga). This species is known to have existed long ago as 35 million years, almost unimaginably longer ago than our own species *Homo sapiens*. Its features bear no overall similarity to any other African mammal, and it constitutes an order all of its own. About the size of a pig, it has an arched back, big upright ears, and a long muzzle with a blunt snout. The short, strong tail is like a kangaroo's in terms of its strength, its use for balance and its function as part of the aardvark's defence mechanism. Each foot, besides having toes (four on the front feet, five on the rear), has a substantial claw which is used for digging and for defence. The aardvark digs with great speed; often the signs of the nightly toil at Lewa Downs are the large holes in the road come morning. Digging is used not only to access food sources (termites and ants, which are "captured" on the long tongue by means of sticky saliva) but to fashion burrows in which to rest or to live for longer periods. The more elaborate burrows are galleried and spread over many hundreds of square metres, with many entrances. It is of great ecological importance that they are often subsequently used as shelter by any number of other species. When the aardvark emerges from its hideout after dark it is notoriously cautious, waiting and listening for many minutes before proceeding with a series of bounds to some 10m from the mouth of its shelter. Thereafter it will range large distances, up to 10km in a single night. Although no extensive research has yet been undertaken into its longevity, the aardvark is known to be long-lived – some in captivity have lived 18 years.

Much more readily visible after dark is the **lesser galago** (*Galago senegalensis*; komba), an endearing arboreal primate, about the size of a squirrel but with more the appearance of a tiny bear. They are extremely vocal and have at least eight distinct calls. One of these is a cry like that of a human infant; this and the large saucer-like eyes are part of their appeal. Galagos (or bushbabies, as they are commonly known) are, perhaps surprisingly, the oldest relatives of homo sapiens. Initially they are easily "caught" in the beam of a spotlight, in which their eyes throw a very bright red reflection. Close-up they can be difficult to pinpoint because they are well camouflaged against the trees – and very small. They use their powerful hind legs to leap up to 7m in a single movement. The bushbaby lives mainly off insects, fruit and seeds and is a popular pet in many parts of Africa, living as long as 14 years.

Not all the mongooses are strictly nocturnal but are grouped together here for the sake of simplicity. The mongooses belong to the sub-family, *Herpestinae*, of the family *Viverridae*, which also includes civets and genets.

MONGOOSE SHAPES

Differentiating between mongooses is often difficult. Other than their social behaviour – some live in packs while others are more solitary - and the fact that some are diurnal, size and shape can be a helpful factor.

Egyptian Mongoose

Marsh Mongoose

White-Tailed Mongoose

Slender Mongoose

Dwarf Mongoose

The **marsh mongoose** (*Atilax paludinosus*; nguchiro) is of robust build with a large head and coarse, shaggy coat. Its relatively short tail is the same brownish colour as the rest of the body. It is almost exclusively nocturnal and usually spotted near water, which provides its diet of freshwater crustaceans, although it will also eat eggs, small birds and frogs. The marsh mongoose is usually solitary. The **Egyptian mongoose** (*Herpestes ichneumon*) is the largest of the mongoose family, growing up to 64cms, and primarily nocturnal. Its grizzled coat of long, coarse hair is of uniform brown-grey colour which, as is the case with all mongooses, varies slightly according to habitat. Its long slender tail has a black tip with a brush-like tassel. It is a very adept tracker, hence its name – *ichneumon* is Greek for tracker. The **white-tailed mongoose** (*Ichneumia albicauda*) is also primarily nocturnal and usually solitary. It is slightly smaller than the other two nocturnal species, but is the most commonly seen at Lewa Downs. It looks rather like a skunk, with a generally grey colouring to its coat and a long, bushy tail. Rather confusingly the tail can be entirely black, although white or off-white is more usual. The limbs appear black.

The two diurnal species found at Lewa Downs are the **slender** (*Herpestes sanguineus*) and **dwarf** (*Helogale parvula*) **mongooses**. The former is yellowish or red-brown, has a long tail with a black tip and is most often seen alone or in a pair. By contrast the dwarf mongoose is gregarious, living in packs of 12-15 which range over very large territories of as much as 30 hectares. These speckled brown or reddish mongooses are the smallest of the family, weighing less than 0.5kg and rarely measuring more than 30cms. They have been the subject of many a documentary on their interesting social life and endearingly perky behaviour. Termite mounds are their favourite lookout posts.

The **civet** (*Viverra civetta*; fungo) looks rather like the American raccoon and is of comparable size. It is famous for the musk that it secretes which has long been used as a base or fixative for flower perfumes. It has a wide range of colourings from buff to dark or yellowish grey with spots, blotches and stripes; there is also a crest of black-tipped hair running from its neck to the tip of the tail. The tail itself is predominantly black, but has 3-4 whitish rings near the base.

Although at first sight it may look like a cat, the **large-spotted genet** (*Genetta tigrina*; kanu) is, like the mongooses and civets, a member of the family *Viverridae*. Long (up to 50cms) and sleek, it has short legs and a small head. Brownish-grey or pale yellowish in colour, its spots are brown or chestnut. Unlike the mongoose or civet it is primarily arboreal, although much of its hunting is done at ground level. The long tail – as long as the body – has 8-9 dark rings and a dark tip. Nocturnal they may be, but they are not shy of residing as close to humans as the verandah roof at Wilderness Trails!

The **caracal's** (*Felis caracal*; simbamangu) most distinctive feature is its long, pointed ears which are topped with a black tassel. The adult caracal is about 45cms high and well-built. It has no readily discernible spots or stripes, the coat being a tawny colour. The caracal likes hilly country and is a very powerful hunter, often preying on animals larger than itself.

The **African wild cat** (*Felis libyca*; paka pori) is shorter than a serval and resembles a domestic tabby cat. Although there is significant variation in colouring, it is altogether greyer than most of the other cats. The ears are also smaller and more pointed. The long tail has several dark rings near its dark tip. Identification is made more difficult by the fact that they interbreed with domestic cats.

A number of the cats are also mainly nocturnal. The graceful **serval** (*Felis serval*; mondo) is the largest of these, standing some 55cms high when fully-grown. Its build, with a small head, long limbs and shortish tail (with black rings) is not unlike that of a cheetah, nor is its relative speed and agility. But with the big, oval ears any similarity ends. These are used for pinpointing prey which the serval will track and then leap on, seizing the victim with both front paws.

The **bat-eared fox** (*Otocyon megalotis*; bweha masigio) is a very small fox, never more than 30cms tall. It has enormous ears which are white inside. The dark colouring around its eyes looks like a highwayman's mask. Its back is a silvery buff colour, making it resemble, ears aside, a small jackal. It mostly feeds off insects and small rodents and inhabits acacia woodland and the plains.

Ratels, zorillas and otters form the family *Mustelidae*, having special scent glands in the perineal region. **Ratels** or **honey-badgers** (*Mellivora capensis*; nyegere) are stout mammals. They are not dissimilar to a European badger with whitish upperparts and pure black sides, underparts and tail. They are extremely fierce and have even been known to attack big game such as buffalo, disabling them by biting or clawing the groin or genitals after which the animal often bleeds to death. Such stories are similar to those of occasional attacks (even on Man) by the European badger. Ratels are very fond of honey and in their pursuit of this delicacy they have a symbiotic relationship with the honey guide (*indicator indicator*). The honey guide leads the ratel which will then break open the hive and share the feast with the bird.

The **zorilla** or **striped polecat** (*Ictonyx striatus*; kicheche) is similar to a skunk, in both size and colouring. It has a long soft coat with a black and white pattern. One of its distinctive features is the white spot on its forehead between the eyes, also the white spot on each cheek. From the nape indistinct black and white stripes stretch to the tail, which is usually all white. It lives primarily on rodents.

Always a fascinating sight is the **crested porcupine** (*Hystrix sp.*; nungu); the porcupine is the largest and heaviest of the African rodents. The young are born with quills which, although they are soft at birth, harden after a few days. When adult these quills are about 30cms long and striped black and white. The eponymous crest is of backward curving bristles on the porcupine's head and neck. If alarmed the quills are raised and vibrated to emit a loud rattling sound. In attack the porcupine will reverse into its target; the quills become easily detached on contact and these lead to festering wounds. Although quills are often to be found on the ground around the ranch porcupines are not, contrary to popular myth, capable of "shooting" the quills. The porcupine is vegetarian and often inhabits aardvark burrows and similar protective shelters.

Another prickly character is the **hedgehog** (*Atelerix pruneri*; kalunguyeye), a close relation of the European species. In Africa it is often attributed mysterious powers; for example, seeds rubbed on the hedgehog's skin are said to be rendered especially fertile. Their benefit to the gardener in suburban habitats is well-known, as slugs and snails form part of their diet.

The Animal Family of Lewa Downs

"Animals are such agreeable friends — they ask no questions, they pass no criticisms".
George Eliot

The animals at Lewa Downs are as special, and as important to the nation and the ecosystem, as anywhere else in the world. Please remember when enjoying watching their unique, and sometimes threatened, patterns of behaviour that they should be allowed to hold sway. Both the animals and their habitats should be regarded as having a very big "DO NOT DISTURB" sign above them. Always follow your guide's advice.

A Living Ranch: Visiting Lewa Downs

FOR MANY this book is intended as a memento of a stay on a very special ranch in an equally special part of Africa. For others it is intended to help in the planning of a visit, and understanding more about what makes Lewa Downs different to so many other game-viewing destinations.

The hundreds of guests who come to stay at Lewa Downs all have a different story to tell of what brought them to this particular corner of Kenya. But one of the common reactions amongst them, other than their enjoyment of the stay, and often in response to a comment overheard just before their departure, was "I had no idea that we could do that here..", or, "I had no idea that that happened here.." This is a tribute to the great breadth of things going on every day, all year round, on the ranch. It is also a tribute to the very relaxed, but enthusiastic, style of Will and Emma Craig and their team, the hosts at Wilderness Trails: they will adapt to make of your stay what you want, and (within reason!) every request is met as a challenge. Such, I feel sure, will also be true of the new Lewa Wildlife Conservancy lodge which is currently being built.

WILDERNESS TRAILS AND THE LWC LODGE

Wilderness Trails is Will and Emma's home. It is an African home. There are dogs who love to be petted; there are tame genets living in the roof above the terrace; there are friendly nannies and cooks and guides. Everything is done to make your stay memorable. The success in achieving this is attested to by the visitors book, and the large number of wildlife enthusiasts who return year after year.

There are only three cottages at Wilderness Trails, each with two double rooms separated by a verandah. As you wake on the first morning and step onto your verandah the cliffs opposite you may already be dotted with game, although you will have to look carefully – the cover is good. Roger, the giraffe, may be sharing the bougainvillea-filled garden with you;

Gilbert and some of his elephant friends may be taking a drink or having a paddle in the stream below; a set of large footprints may be visible as a reminder that they passed quite close by in the night, but in total silence. Behind you, in the clear sky of the early morning, Mount Kenya rises from the surrounding foothills. In the yard, out of earshot, Lewa Downs is already alive: the horses are frisky after their night of confinement; the carpenters are fashioning a new chair or table or carving another striking statue; the girls are already hard at work in the carpet workshop. And breakfast is on the table, the first of many sumptuous meals all made with produce grown on the ranch. The water in your bathroom comes fresh from a spring; it is heated using dead firewood. Lewa Downs is very much in harmony with of its surroundings. It is open all year round with the exception of the rainy seasons in April and November.

You can set your own pace, and everyone's programme is individually tailored. Choose from game drives, by day or by night; horse riding, on very docile steeds, that facilitate extraordinary proximity to the plains game; walks, with an ornithological expert around Wilderness Trails, or up in the Ngare Ndare forest, or with David Craig to bring to life the prehistoric sites; visits to Anna Merz, one of the foremost authorities on rhinos, and her charges; or a night spent camping in the open. Alternatively explore working aspects of the ranch: the ranch itself, the painstaking security arrangements, the furniture workshop or the carpet weaving or the group ranch at Ilngwesi. Lewa Downs is also close enough to try a shopping trip to nearby Isiolo, a trading town with all the colour and vitality that one would expect of an outpost with such a strong Somali influence. It is also a useful base for camel safaris to the north, or fishing trips on Mount Kenya. But then again, you might just prefer to sit on the lawn with a glass of fruit juice squeezed only minutes before and take in the sights, sounds and smells of Africa more effortlessly.

KIFUMA CARPETS

"Kifuma" means "a community woven together". A new expanded workshop has recently been constructed within walking distance of Wilderness Trails, to meet demand for the beautiful carpets it produces. Using traditional Ethiopian techniques some twenty girls from the surrounding area weave the carpets in ivories, browns and misty greys from wool bought from neighbouring small-scale sheep farmers. The wool is first sorted into colours, then spun, plied, washed, mothproofed, sundried and woven on handmade cedar looms. The spinning shed is a hive of activity, often accompanied by singing. The employment of so many is important in an area where prospects for jobs are not great; the system is "piecework", that is to say the girls can take leave of absence, for instance for childbirth, and their job will await them. The carpets, measuring anything from 2ft x 3ft to 10ft x 16ft, and with a variety of designs – often featuring wildlife – are exported all over the world. Women's groups are also organised in the locality; these are used as a forum offering advice on anything from setting up a water-tank, to ideas for fuel saving, to family matters.

A Living Ranch: Visiting Lewa Downs

FURNITURE WORKSHOP

A number of skilled craftsmen work producing anything from traditional Kenyan carvings to "Lamu-style" chairs, beds and tables to faithful reproductions of European designs. Some acacia from the ranch itself is used, for example for bowls and picture frames; camphor and rosewoods from Mount Kenya are also used in furniture manufacture. In each case the trees chosen are past seeding age in order to minimise environmental damage. Although in its infancy, the very high standard of work has attracted much attention; as with the carpets much of the finished product goes abroad.

SCHOOLS

Local schooling is one of the vital institutions that Lewa Downs seeks to support. There are four schools nearby. The Elizabeth Foundation was encouraged to help with infrastructure developments (although the government will provide teachers, the parents have to provide the classrooms and this is often beyond their means); Andy Lodge at H.O.R.N., the Lewa Wildlife Conservancy/Ngare Sergoi Rhino Sanctuary support group, lectures to the schools and collects useful materials for them from all over the USA; a penpal network, between local and American children has also been started. Visits to the ranch by local children are regularly organised to promote awareness of wildlife conservation issues. In addition a number of bursaries are offered to pupils, to pay for their secondary schooling. Among the past beneficiaries of this system is John Kikaru, who now runs the Lewa Wildlife Conservancy office. A visit to one of the schools can easily be arranged. The wonderfully pithy observations on animals in the previous chapter are from children at local schools.

EDUCATION CENTRE

Plans are well advanced to start an Education Centre on the ranch itself.

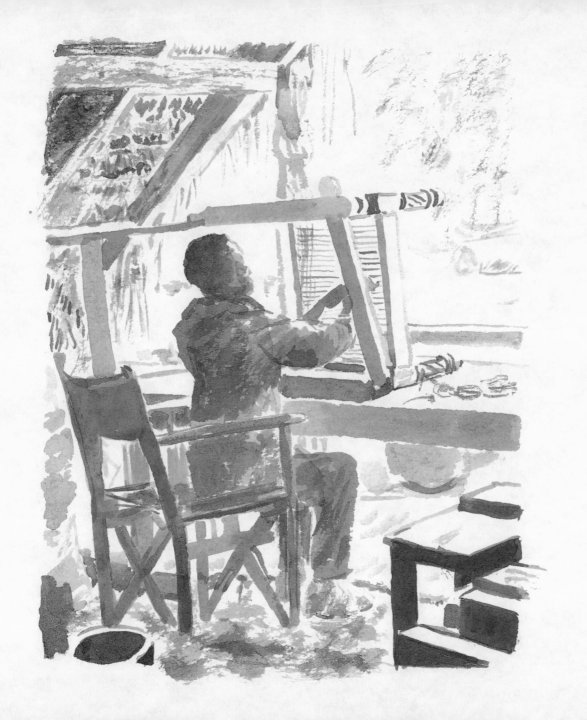

Larger Mammal Checklist

SPECIES

- AARDWOLF
- AARDVARK
- BABOON, OLIVE
- BUFFALO, CAPE
- BUSHBUCK
- CARACAL
- CHEETAH
- CIVET
- DIKDIK
- DUIKER
- ELAND, EAST AFRICAN
- ELEPHANT
- FOX, BAT-EARED
- GALAGO, LESSER
- GAZELLE, GRANT'S
- GENET, LARGE-SPOTTED
- GERENUK
- GIRAFFE, RETICULATED
- HARE, CRAWSHAY'S
- HARTEBEEST, KENYA
- HEDGEHOG
- HYAENA, SPOTTED
- HYAENA, STRIPED
- HYRAX, ROCK
- HYRAX, BUSH
- IMPALA
- JACKAL, BLACK-BACKED
- JACKAL, SIDE-STRIPED
- KLIPSPRINGER
- KUDU, GREATER

- LEOPARD
- LION
- MONGOOSE, DWARF
- MONGOOSE, EGYPTIAN
- MONGOOSE, MARSH
- MONGOOSE, SLENDER
- MONGOOSE, WHITE-TAILED
- MONKEY, COLOBUS
- MONKEY, PATAS
- MONKEY, SYKES
- MONKEY, VERVET
- ORYX
- OSTRICH, SOMALI
- OSTRICH, MAASAI
- OTTER, CAPE CLAWLESS
- PORCUPINE, CRESTED
- RATEL
- REEDBUCK, MOUNTAIN
- RHINOCEROS, WHITE
- RHINOCEROS, BLACK
- SITATUNGA
- SERVAL
- STEENBOK
- WATERBUCK, COMMON
- WATERBUCK, DEFASSA
- WARTHOG
- WILD CAT
- ZEBRA, COMMON
- ZEBRA, GREVY'S
- ZORILLA

Of course animals come and animals go; if you should see a species not listed here please tell either Ian or William Craig so that it can be added to the list.

Lewa Downs Bird Checklist

THERE IS a tremendous variety of birds to be seen at Lewa Downs. This is a function of the variety of habitats, ranging from the swamp area to the river valleys; from the open grasslands to the cliffs of the rocky outcrops and, of course, the adjacent Ngare Ndare forest. If birding is your particular interest there are expert guides to help you. There is no reason to believe that this list is comprehensive. You may well spot species never seen before, which adds to the fun. If so please report it so that the list can be constantly updated.

KEY TO SPECIES
r = resident
c = common
pm = paleartic migrant
lm = local migrant
vr = very rare

The following birds were recorded at Lewa Downs between January 1984 and the present day.

STRUTHIONIDAE ostriches

ostrich	*struthio camelus* **r**

PELECANIDAE pelicans

great white pelican	*pelecanus onocrotalus* **lm**
pink-backed pelican	*pelecanus rufescens* **lm**

CICONIIDAE storks

marabou stork	*leptoptilos crumeniferus* **lm**
saddlebill stork	*ephippiorhynchus senegalensis* **vr**
yellow-billed stork	*ibis ibis* **c**
European white stork	*ciconia ciconia* **pm**

Lewa Downs Bird Checklist

European black stork	*ciconia nigra* **pm**
woolly-necked stork	*ciconia episcopus* **vr**
Abdim's stork	*ciconia abdimii* **vr**
openbill stork	*anastomus lamelligerus* **vr**

THRESKIORNITHIDAE ibises, spoonbills

hadada ibis	*hagedashia hagedash* **r**
sacred ibis	*threskiornis aethiopicus* **lm**
glossy ibis	*plegadis falcinellus* **vr**
African spoonbill	*platalea alba* **lm**

ARDEIDAE herons, egrets, bitterns

great white heron	*egretta alba* **lm**
grey heron	*ardea cinerea* **r**
black-headed heron	*ardea melanocephela* **r**
night heron	*nycticorx nycticorax* **vr**
squacco heron	*ardeola ralloides* **r**
green-backed heron	*butorides striatus* **r**
cattle egret	*ardeola ibis* **c**
little egret	*egretta garzetta* **vr**
yellow-billed egret	*egretta intermedia* **vr**
little bittern	*ixobrychus minutus* **vr**
dwarf bittern	*ardeirallus sturmii* **vr**

SCOPIDAE hamerkop

hammerkop	*scopus umbretta* **r**

BALEARICIDAE cranes

crowned crane	*balearica regulorum* **r**

PHOENICOPTERIDAE flamingos

lesser flamingo	*phoenicopterus minor* **vr**

PHALACROCORACIDAE cormorants

white-necked cormorant	*phalacrocorax carbo* **lm**
long-tailed cormorant	*phalacrocorax aficanus* **lm**

ANATIDAE ducks, geese

spur-winged goose	*plectropterus gambensis* **lm**
Egyptian Goose	*alopochen aegyptiaca* **r**
knob-billed duck	*sarkidiornis melanotos* **lm**
fulvous tree duck	*dendrocygna bicolor* **vr**
European pintail	*anas acuta* **pm**
African black duck	*anas sparsa* **r**
yellow-billed duck	*anas undulata* **r**
red-billed duck	*anas erythrorhynchos* **r**
Hottentot teal	*anas hottentota* **lm**
African pochard	*aythya erythrophthalma* **lm**
Maccoa duck	*oxyura maccoa* **lm**

RALLIDAE coots, rails, crakes

red-knobbed coot	*fulica cristata* **c**
common moorhen	*gallinula chloropus* **c**
black crake	*limnocorax flavirostra* **r**

PODICIPIDAE grebes, dabchicks

great crested grebe	*podiceps cristatus* **vr**
little grebe	*podiceps ruficollis* **c**

ANHINGIDAE darters

African darter	*anhinga rufa* **vr**

ACCIPITRIDAE vultures, eagles, hawks

Nubian vulture	*torgos tracheliotus* **lm**
Rueppels vulture	*gyps rueppelli*
white backed vulture	*gyps bengalensis* **lm**
hooded vulture	*necrosyrtes monachus* **vr**
Egyptian vulture	*neophron percnopterus* **vr**
Martial eagle	*polemaetus bellicosus* **r**
spotted eagle	*aquila clanga* **pm**
tawny eagle	*aquila rapax* **c**
Verreaux's eagle	*aquila verreauxii* **vr**
Wahlberg's eagle	*aquila wahlbergi* **vr**

African fish eagle	*haliaeetus vocifer* **vr**
bateleur	*terathopius ecaudatus* **c**
gymnogene	*polyboroides radiatus* **lm**
osprey	*pandion haliaetus* **vr**
African hawk eagle	*hieraaetus spilogaster* **r**
black-chested harrier eagle	*circaetus pectoralis* **c**
brown harrier eagle	*circaetus cinereus* **lm**
long-crested eagle	*lophaetus occipitalis* **vr**
augur buzzard	*buteo rufofuscus* **lm**
steppe buzzard	*buteo buteo* **pm**
lizard buzzard	*kaupifalco monogrammicus* **vr**
pallid harrier	*circus macrourus* **pm**
Montagu's harrier	*circus pygargus* **pm**
African goshawk	*accipiter tachiro* **c**
great sparrowhawk	*accipiter melanoleucus* **vr**
little sparrowhawk	*accipiter minullus* **c**
pale chanting goshawk	*melierax poliopterus* **r**
Gabar goshawk	*melierax gabar* **r**
black kite	*milvus migrans* **lm**
black-shouldered kite	*elanus caerulus* **lm**
swallow-tailed kite	*chelictinia riocourii* **lm**

SAGITTARIIDAE secretary bird

secretary bird	*sagittarius serpentarius* **lm**

FALCONIDAE falcons

grey kestrel	*falco ardosiaceus* **vr**
lanner	*falco biarmicus* **lm**
African hobby	*falco cuvieri* **pm**
European lesser kestrel	*falco naumanni* **pm**
peregrine	*falco peregrinus* **lm**
kestrel	*falco tinnunculus* **r**
pygmy falcon	*poliohierax semitorquatus* **c**

PHASIANIDAE guineafowl, francolins, quails

vulturine guineafowl	*acryllium vulturinum* **vr**
helmeted guineafowl	*numida meleagris* **r**

stone partridge	*ptilopachus petrosus* **r**
yellow-necked spurfowl	*francolinus leucoscepus* **r**
scaly francolin	*francolinus squamatus* **vr**
coqui francolin	*francolinus coqui* **c**
crested francolin	*francolinus sephaena* **r**
harlequin quail	*coturnix delegorguei* **lm**

TURNICIDAE buttonquail

button quail	*turnix sylvatica* **lm**

OTIDIDAE bustards

kori bustard	*ardeotis kori* **r**
black-bellied bustard	*eupodotis melanogaster* **r**
Hartlaub's bustard	*eupodotis hartlaubii* **vr**
buff-crested bustard	*eupodotis ruficrista* **vr**
white-bellied bustard	*eupodotis senegalensis* **r**

JACANIDAE lily-trotters

lily trotter	*actophilornis africanus* **vr**

BURHINIDAE stone curlews or thicknees

spotted stone curlew	*burhinus capensis* **r**
european stone curlew	*burhinus oedicnemus* **pm**
Senegal stone curlew	*burhinus senegalensis* **lm**
water dikkop	*burhinus vermiculatus* **lm**

RECURVIROSTRIDAE stilts, avocets

black-winged stilt	*himantopus himantopus* **pm**
avocet	*recurvirostra avosetta* **pm**

SCOLOPACIDAE snipe, sandpipers, stints

European common snipe	*gallinago gallinago* **pm**
black-tailed godwit	*limosa limosa* **pm**
greenshank	*tringa nebularia* **pm**
redshank	*tringa totanus* **pm**
spotted redshank	*tringa erythropus* **pm**

wood sandpiper	*tringa glareola* **pm**
common sandpiper	*tringa hypoleucos* **pm**
green sandpiper	*tringa ochropus* **pm**
marsh sandpiper	*tringa stagnatilis* **pm**
curlew sandpiper	*calidris ferruginea* **pm**
broad-billed sandpiper	*limicola falcinellus* **pm**
little stint	*calidris minuta* **pm**
Temminck's stint	*calidris temminckii* **pm**

CHARADRIIDAE plovers

crowned plover	*vanellus coronatus* **r**
black-winged plover	*vanellus melanopterus* **lm**
blacksmith plover	*vanellus armatus* **r**
spur-winged plover	*vanellus spinosus* **r**
three-banded plover	*charadrius tricollaris* **lm**
Kittlitz's plover	*charadrius pecuarius* **lm**

GLAREOLIDAE coursers

Temminck's courser	*cursorius temminckii* **lm**
two-banded courser	*hemerodromus africanus* **lm**
Heuglin's courser	*hemerodromus cinctus* **lm**

LARIDAE gulls

grey-headed gulls	*larus cirrocephalus* **lm**

STERNIDAE terns

gull-billed tern	*gelochelidon nilotica* **pm**

PTEROCLIDIDAE sandgrouse

Lichtenstein's sandgrouse	*pterocles lichtensteini* **r**
chestnut-bellied sandgrouse	*pterocles exustus* **lm**
black-faced sandgrouse	*pterocles decoratus* **lm**

COLUMBIDAE pigeons, doves

olive pigeon	*columba arquatrix* **lm**
speckled pigeon	*columba guinea* **r**
namaqua dove	*oena capensis* **lm**
ring–necked dove	*streptopelia capicola* **r**
red–eyed dove	*streptopelia semitorquata* **r**
laughing dove	*streptopelia senegalensis* **r**
pink–breasted dove	*streptopelia lugens* **lm**
emerald–spotted wood dove	*turtur chalcospilos* **r**
tambourine dove	*turtur tympanistria* **vr**

PSITTACIDAE parrots

orange–billed parrot	*poicephalus rufiventris* **r**
brown parrot	*poicephalus meyeri* **lm**

MUSOPHAGIDAE go–away birds, turacos

white–bellied go–away bird	*corythaixoides leucogaster* **r**
Hartlaub's turaco	*tauraco hartlaubi* **vr**

TROGONIDAE trogons

Narina's trogon	*apaloderma narina* **vr**

BUCEROTIDAE hornbills

crowned hornbill	*tockus alboterminatus* **c**
Von der Decken's hornbill	*tockus deckeni* **r**
yellow–billed hornbill	*tockus flavirostris* **c**
red–billed hornbill	*tockus erythrorhynchus* **r**
grey hornbill	*tockus nasutus* **c**

CUCULIDAE coucals, cuckoos

white–browed coucal	*centropus superciliosus* **r**
great spotted cuckoo	*culculus glandarius* **pm**
red–chested cuckoo	*culculus solitarius* **lm**
black–and–white (Jacobin) cuckoo	*culculus jacobinus* **lm**
european cuckoo	*culculus canorus* **pm**

striped cuckoo	*culculus levaillantii* **lm**
black cuckoo	*culculus clamosus* **lm**
Didric cuckoo	*chrysococcyx caprius* **lm**
Klaas's cuckoo	*chrysococcyx klaas*

STRIGIDAE owls

African barn owl	*tyto alba* **vr**
African marsh owl	*asio capensis* **vr**
Verreaux's eagle owl	*bubo lacteus* **r**
spotted eagle owl	*bubo africanus* **vr**
Pel's fishing owl	*scotopelia peli* **vr**
white-faced scops owl	*otus leucotis* **vr**
African scops owl	*otus scops*
pearl-spotted owlet	*glaucidium perlatum* **c**

CAPRIMULGIDAE nightjars

Donaldson-Smith's nightjar	*caprimulgus donaldsoni* **c**
Mozambique nightjar	*caprimulgus clarus* **lm**
standard-winged nightjar	*macrodipteryx longipennis* **lm**

CORVIDAE crows, ravens

pied crow	*corvus albus* **vr**
fan-tailed raven	*corvus rhipidurus* **c**

STURNIDAE starlings, oxpeckers

violet-backed starling	*cinnyricinclus leucogaster* **lm**
wattled starling	*creatophora cinerea* **lm**
blue-eared glossy starling	*lamprotornis chalybeus* **r**
Hildebrandt's starling	*spreo hildebrandti* **r**
superb starling	*spreo superbus* **c**
yellow-billed oxpecker	*buphagus africanus* **r**

ORIOLIDAE orioles

black-headed oriole	*oriolus larvatus* **r**
European golden oriole	*oriolus oriolus* **pm**

DICRURIDAE drongos

African drongo   *dicrurus adsimilis* **c**

APODIDAE swifts, spinetails

mottled swift   *apus aequatorialis* **lm**
little swift   *apus affinis* **lm**
European swift   *apus apus* **pm**
white-rumped swift   *apus caffer* **r**
Nyanza swift   *apus niansae* **lr**
Boehm's spinetail   *neafrapus boehmi* **lm**

HIRUNDINIDAE swallows, martins

striped swallow   *hirundo abyssinica* **vr**
Ethiopian swallow   *hirundo aethiopica* **lm**
European swallow   *hirundo rustica* **pm**
Red-rumped swallow   *hirundo daurica* **lm**
African Rock martin   *hirundo fuligula* **lm**
black roughwing swallow   *psalidoprocne holomelaena* **lm**
banded martin   *riparia cincta* **vr**

CORACIIDAE rollers

lilac-breasted roller   *coracias caudata* **r**
European roller   *coracias garrulus* **pm**
rufous-crowned roller   *coracias naevia* **lr**
broad-billed roller   *eurystomus glaucurus* **vr**

UPUPIDAE hoopoes

hoopoe   *upupa epops africana* **c**

PHOENICULIDAE wood hoopoes, scimitarbills

violet wood hoopoe   *phoeniculus damarensis* **r**
african scimitarbill   *phoeniculus cyanomelas* **vr**
Abyssinian scimitarbill   *phoeniculus minor* **lr**

Lewa Downs Bird Checklist

MEROPIDAE bee-eaters

European bee-eater	*merops apiaster* **pm**
cinnamon-chested bee-eater	*merops oreobates* **r**
Madagascar bee-eater	*merops superciliosis* **lm**
blue-cheeked bee-eater	*merops persicus* **lm**
little bee-eater	*merops pusillus* **r**

ALCEDINIDAE kingfishers

giant kingfisher	*ceryle maxima* **vr**
pied kingfisher	*ceryle rudis* **c**
striped kingfisher	*halcyon chelicuti* **c**
grey-headed kingfisher	*halcyon leucocephala* **c**

CAPITONIDAE barbets, tinkerbirds

red and yellow barbet	*trachyphonus erythrocephalis* **c**
D'Arnaud's barbet	*trachyphonus darnaudii* **c**
red-fronted barbet	*tricholaema diadematum* **c**
spotted-flanked barbet	*tricholaema lacrymosum* **r**
red-fronted tinkerbird	*pogoniulus pusillus* **c**

PICIDAE woodpeckers

Nubian woodpecker	*campethera nubica* **c**
Cardinal woodpecker	*dendropicos fuscescens* **c**
grey woodpecker	*mesopicos goertae* **c**
bearded woodpecker	*thripias namaquus* **c**

INDICATORIDAE honeyguides

greater honeyguide	*indicator indicator* **c**
lesser honeyguide	*indiator minor* **c**
scaly-throated honeyguide	*indicator variegatus* **c**

COLIIDAE mousebirds

speckled mousebird	*colius striatus* **c**
blue-naped mousebird	*urocolius macrourus* **c**

ALAUDIDAE larks

rufous-naped lark	*mirafra africana* **r**
fawn-coloured lark	*mirafra africanoides* **r**
northern white-tailed lark	*mirafra albicauda* **lm**
flappet lark	*mirafra rufocinnamomea* **vr**
Fischer's sparrow lark	*eremopterix leucopareia* **c**
chestnut-backed sparrow lark	*eremopterix leucotis* **c**

MOTACILLIDAE pipits, wagtails, longclaws

European tree pipit	*anthus trivialis* **pm**
Richard's pipit	*anthus novaeseelandiae* **lm**
plain-backed pipit	*anthus leucophrys* **lm**
sandy plain-backed pipit	*anthus vaalensis* **r**
African pied wagtail	*motacilla aguimp* **r**
European grey wagtail	*motacilla cinerea* **pm**
yellow wagtail	*motacilla flava* **pm**
mountain wagtail	*motacilla clara* **lm**
yellow-throated longclaw	*macronyx croceus* **vr**
rosy-breasted longclaw	*macronyx ameliae* **vr**
Pangani lonclaw	*macronyx aurantiigula* **vr**

PYCNONOTIDAE bulbuls

yellow-vented bulbul	*pycnonotus barbatus* **r**

TURDOIDIDAE chatterers, babblers

rufous chatterer	*argya rubiginosa* **r**
black-lored babbler	*turdoides melanops* **r**

TURDIDAE thrushes, wheatears, robins, chats

olive thrush	*turdus olivaceus* **vr**
Kurrichane thrush	*turdus libonyanus* **vr**
European Rock thrush	*monticola saxatilis* **pm**
Isabelline wheatear	*oenanthe isabellina* **pm**
common wheatear	*oenanthe oenanthe* **pm**
pied wheatear	*oenanthe leucomela* **pm**

Lewa Downs Bird Checklist

desert wheatear	*oenanthe deserti* **pm**
Schalow's wheatear	*oenanthe lugubris* **vr**
white-winged scrub robin	*erythrina leucoptera* **vr**
robin chat	*cossypha caffra* **c**
white-browed robin chat	*cossypha semirufa* **c**
red-tailed chat	*cercomela familiaris* **c**
anteater chat	*myrmecocichla aethiops* **vr**
stonechat	*saxicola torquata* **pm**
cliffchat	*thamnolea cinnamomeiventris* **vr**

CAMPEPHAGIDAE cuckoo shrikes

black cuckoo shrike	*campephaga sulphurata* **vr**

PRIONOPIDAE helmet shrikes

straight-crested helmet shrike	*prionops plumata* **c**
white-crowned shrike	*eurocephalus ruppelli* **r**

LANIIDAE shrikes, fiscals, bush shrikes, puffbacks, boubous, brubrus, tchagras

fiscal shrike	*lanius collaris* **vr**
Taita fiscal	*lanius dorsalis* **r**
lesser grey shrike	*lanius minor* **pm**
rufous red-tailed shrike	*lanius cristatus phoenicusvides* **pm**
red-tailed shrike	*lanius cristatus* **pm**
red-backed shrike	*lanius colluria* **pm**
rosy-patched shrike	*rhodophoneus cruentus* **pm**
grey-headed bush shrike	*malaconotus blanchoti* **vr**
sulphur-breasted bush shrike	*malaconotus sulfureopectus* **vr**
black-backed puffback	*dryoscopus cubla* **c**
tropical boubou	*laniarius ferrugineus* **r**
slate-coloured boubou	*laniarius funebris* **r**
Northern brubru	*nilaus afer* **c**
three-streaked tchagra	*tchagra jamesi* **r**
black-headed tchagra	*tchagra senegala* **vr**

MUSCICAPIDAE flycatchers

white-eyed slaty flycatcher	*dioptrornis fischeri* **c**

black flycatcher	*melaenornis pammelaina* **r**
grey flycatcher	*bradornis microrhynchus* **c**
pale flycatcher	*bradornis pallidus* **vr**
dusky flycatcher	*alseonax adustus* **c**
european spotted flycatcher	*muscicapa striata* **pm**
paradise flycatcher	*terpsiphone viridis* **c**
chin-spot flycatcher	*batis molitor* **c**
silverbird	*empidornis semipartitus* **vr**

SYLVIIDAE warblers, camaropteras, prinias, apalisis, eremomelas, cisticolas, crombecs

banded tit-warbler	*parisoma bohmi* **c**
european reed warbler	*acrocephalus scirpaceus* **pm**
European sedge warbler	*acrocephalus schoenobaenus* **pm**
olive-tree warbler	*hippolais olivetorum* **pm**
willow warbler	*phylloscopus trochilus* **pm**
garden warbler	*sylvia borin* **pm**
blackcap warbler	*sylvia atricapilla* **pm**
spotted morning warbler	*cichladusa guttata* **vr**
grey wren warbler	*camaroptera simplex* **vr**
grey-backed camaroptera	*camaroptera brevicaudata* **r**
tawny-flanked prinia	*prinia subflava* **c**
black-breasted apalis	*apalis flavida* **vr**
yellow-bellied eremomela	*eremomela icteropygialis* **c**
ashy cisticola	*cisticola cinereola* **c**
pectoral-patch cisticola	*cisticola brunnescens* **r**
rattling cisticola	*cisticola chiniana* **r**
croaking cisticola	*cisticola natalensis* **c**
stout cisticola	*cisticola robusta* **c**
red-faced crombec	*sylvietta whytii* **c**
crombec	*sylvietta brachyura* **c**

ZOSTEROPIDAE white-eyes

Kikuyu white-eye	*zosterops kikuyuensis* **vr**

PARIDAE tits

grey tit	*parus afer* **vr**
white-breasted tit	*parus albiventris* **c**

Lewa Downs Bird Checklist

NECTARINIIDAE sunbirds

amethyst sunbird	*nectarinia amethystina* **vr**
mariqua sunbird	*nectarinia mariquensis* **r**
scarlet-chested sunbird	*nectarinia senegalensis* **r**
variable sunbird	*nectarinia venusta* **vr**
bronze sunbird	*nectarinia kilimensis* **vr**
malachite sunbird	*nectarinia famosa* **vr**
Hunter's sunbird	*nectarinia hunteri* **vr**
green-throated sunbird	*nectarinia rubescens* **vr**
Kenya violet-backed sunbird	*anthreptes orientalis* **vr**

PLOCEIDAE weavers, bishops, widowbirds, whydahs, sparrows, queleas

red-billed buffalo weaver	*bubalornis niger* **vr**
white-headed buffalo weaver	*dinemellia dinemelli* **c**
white-browed sparrow weaver	*plocepasser mahali* **r**
red-headed weaver	*anaplectes rubriceps* **r**
Reichenow's weaver	*ploceus baglafecht reichenowi* **r**
Layard's black-headed weaver	*ploceus cucullatus nigriceps* **c**
masked weaver	*ploceus intermedius* **vr**
spectacled weaver	*ploceus ocularis* **vr**
chestnut weaver	*ploceus rubiginosus* **lm**
speke's weaver	*ploceus spekei* **r**
vitelline masked weaver	*ploceus velatus* **c**
Holub's golden weaver	*ploceus xanthops* **vr**
black-capped social weaver	*pseudonigrita cabanisi* **c**
grey-headed social weaver	*pseudonigrita arnaudi* **r**
yellow bishop	*euplectus capensis* **vr**
long-tailed widowbird	*euplectus progne* **lm**
Jackson's widowbird	*euplectus jacksoni* **lm**
white-winged widowbird	*euplectus albonotatus* **lm**
paradise whydah	*steganura paradisaea* **vr**
pin-tailed whydah	*vidua macroura* **c**
straw-tailed whydah	*vidua fischeri* **c**
chestnut sparrow	*passer eminbey* **lm**
grey-headed sparrow	*passer griseus* **r**
rufous sparrow	*passer motitensis* **r**
Sudan golden sparrow	*fringilla lutea* **vr**

yellow-spotted petronia	*petronia xanthosterna* **c**
indigo-bird	*hypochera chalybeata* **vr**
red-billed quelea	*quelea quelea* **lm**

EMBERIZIDAE buntings

| golden-breasted bunting | *emberiza flaviventris* **vr** |
| cinnamon-breasted rock bunting | *emberiza tahapisi* **r** |

FRINGILLIDAE finches

streaky seed-eater	*serinus striolatus* **vr**
yellow-rumped seed-eater	*serinus atrogularis* **r**
brimstone canary	*serinus sulphuratus* **c**
yellow-fronted canary	*serinus mozambicus* **vr**
white-bellied canary	*serinus dorsostriatus* **vr**
African citril	*serinus citrinelloides* **vr**

ESTRILDIDAE waxbills

quailfinch	*ortygospiza atricollis* **vr**
red-billed firefinch	*lagonosticta senegala* **r**
red-cheeked cordon-bleu	*uraeginthus bengalus* **r**
purple grenadier	*uraeginthus ianthinogaster* **r**
cut-throat amadina	*fasciata* **c**
crimson-rumped waxbill	*estrilda rhodopyga* **c**
lavender waxbill	*estrilda perreini* **vr**
silverbill	*euodice malabarica* **vr**
grey-headed silverbill	*odontospiza caniceps* **vr**

The Collins Field Guide to the Birds of East Africa is a good reference book to carry with you.

Practical Information: useful addresses

For further information about organising a visit to Lewa Downs contact:

IN THE UK

Abercrombie & Kent Ltd.
Sloane Square House
Holbein Place
London SW1W 8NS

Tel: 0171 730 9600
Fax: 0171 730 9376

Worldwide Journeys & Expeditions Limited
8 Comeragh Rd
London W14 9HP

Tel: 0171 381 8638
Fax: 0171 381 0836

Ker & Downey
18 Albermarle St
London W1X 3HA

Tel: 0171 629 2044
Fax: 0171 491 9177

IN KENYA

Chris Flatt
Bush Homes of East Africa
PO Box 56923
Nairobi

Tel: 254 2 506139
Fax: 254 2 502739

IN THE USA

Abercrombie & Kent Overseas Ltd
1520 Kensington Rd
Suite 201
Oakbrook
Illinois 60521

Tel: 708 954 4758
Fax: 708 954 2814

Bush Homes of East Africa
1786-A Century Boulevard
Atlanta
Georgia 30345

Tel: 404 325 5088
Fax: 404 315 9809

Ker & Downey Inc
13201 NW Freeway
Suite 850
Houston
Texas 77040

Tel: 713 744 5260
Fax: 713 895 8753

Rafiki Safaris
45 Rawson Avenue
Camden
Maine 04843

Tel: 207 236 4244
Fax: 207 236 6253

Charities and support groups especially involved with the work of the Ngare Sergoi Rhino Sanctuary, and who publish regular newsletters, include:

H.O.R.N.
PO Box 29503
Columbus, Ohio 43229, USA

Rhino Trust
4045 N.Massachusetts, Portland
Oregon 97227, USA

East African Wildlife Society ("EAWS")
PO Box 20110, Nairobi, KENYA

Please write to them for further details.

FOR THE CAUSE....

The sum of $3 will be donated by the publishers to the Lewa Wildlife Conservancy for each copy of this publication sold, in order to assist in the funding of conservation work undertaken at Lewa Downs.

NEW DEVELOPMENTS

Life at Lewa Downs changes continually. One of the more exciting new developments is that a new lodge, under the management of the Lewa Wildlife Conservancy, is now under construction. Given the size of the ranch, and the fact that only twelve guests at a time can be accommodated at Wilderness Trails, numbers on the ranch will remain strictly limited.

USEFUL FIELD GUIDES:

Dorst,J. and Dandelot,P.
"A Field Guide to the Larger Mammals of Africa"
Publisher: Collins
ISBN: 0 00 219294 2

Williams, J.G. and Arlott,N.
"A Field Guide to the Birds of East Africa"
Publisher: Collins
ISBN: 0 00 219179 2

Estes, Richard D.
"The Safari Companion"
Publisher: Chelsea Green Publishing Company
ISBN: 0 930031 49 0

Blundell,M.
"Wild Flowers of East Africa"
Publisher: Collins
ISBN: 0 00 219812 6

A comprehensive reading list, or advice on background reading, on Africa in general, and Kenya in particular, can be provided by:

Rafiki Books
45 Rawson Avenue, Camden, Maine 04843, USA

Tel: 207 236 4244
Fax: 207 236 6253

The Travel Bookshop
13 Blenheim Crescent, London W11 1EA

Tel: 0171 229 5260

Pan Bookshop
158 Fulham Road, London SW10 9PG

Tel: 0171 393 4997

Africa Book Centre
38 King St, London WC2

Tel: 0171 240 6649

Bibliography

By the very nature of this book, much of the research has been conducted orally. I am particularly grateful to David and Delia Craig, Ian and Jane Craig, William and Emma Craig, David and Susan Brown, Anna Merz, Peter and Sarah Jenkins, Charlie and Carol Wheeler, Don Young, Chief Simon Kinyaga, and all the guides and LWC staff on Lewa Downs. In addition the following texts were invaluable background reading:

PUBLISHED:

R. Estes	*The Safari Companion*
A. Fedders	*Peoples And Cultures Of Kenya*
G. Hanley	*Year Of The Lion*
A.C. Hollis	*The Masai: Their Language and Folklore*
E. Huxley	*Nine Faces of Kenya*
R. Leakey	*The Making Of Mankind*
E. O'Brien	*What Was The Acheulean Hand Axe*
A. Merz	*Rhino At The Brink Of Extinction*
C. Moss	*Elephant Memories*
L. Powys	*Black Laughter*
E. Trzebinski	*The Kenya Pioneers*

1994 WWF Species Status Report: *Rhinos In The Wild*

UNPUBLISHED:

J. Foster	*The Settlement Of Timau 1910-1940*
L. Linson **W. Giesen**	*An Ecological Study Of Lewa Downs*
M. Pickford	*The Prehistory Of Lewa Downs*
S. Rottcher	*Zur Abundanz Grosser Herbivorer Auf Einer "Cattle Ranch" in Kenia*

Conservation Strategy And Management Plan For The Black Rhino Species In Kenya (KWS/Zoological Society Of London)

Index

Index